Cataloochee Cooking

2nd Edition
by Judy Alexander Coker

ISBN 0-9669289-6-2

Visit Cataloochee Ranch website
at www.cataloochee-ranch.com
or call 828.926.1401 for additional
Cataloochee Cooking books or to order
a copy of *Mountain Fever*, a chronicle
of one man's love affair with a region
and a dream.

Coordinated by The Laser Image, Inc.
    Asheville, NC

Printed by Keen Impressions
    Asheville, NC

Graphic Design by Susan Rhew Design, Inc.
    Asheville, NC

Cover photograph and select chapter-head
photographs by Benjamin Porter with the
accompaniment of photo-stylist Jodee Mitchell
and art director Susan Rhew.

*At Three Forks, Mr. Tom's and
Miss Judy's first foray into the
hospitality industry, fresh mountain
trout was the favorite supper.
This string was cataloged by
George Masa, the noted Japanese-
American photographer who took
his evocative pictures while measuring Smoky Mountain trails by
pushing the front end of a bicycle
complete with a pedometer.*

Cataloochee Cooking

This revision of *Cataloochee Cooking* is long overdue. I wrote the first little book in 1990 and revised it in 1994. Now is the time to add new recipes and modify old ones, provide a section about our popular Cataloochee Ranch cookouts and update family lore.

This book could not have been done without advice and editing help from sister-in-law, Jane Alexander, an experienced journalist who worked for many years at the old *LIFE Magazine* and *Time-Life Books* before becoming a senior editor at *Science 80*. Sister Alice, with her usual flair, consulted on pictures, recipes and format and made sense of the Alexander family tree. Other family members and friends on and off the mountain, including Cataloochee Colonists who live here part of the year, have enriched the book by contributing recipes and ideas.

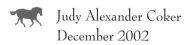 Judy Alexander Coker
December 2002

FROM TOP: *Riders raring to go on the first American Forestry Association pack trip in 1935.*
Putting up the hay — the old-timey way.

Contents

Introduction

Cataloochee Ranch cooking today is the outcome of a selection process that has been underway for more than 80 years. Rooted in my mother's Tidewater Virginia upbringings, it has been vastly enriched by strains from the mountains, a succession of chefs, and even from thoughtful guests who stuck their heads in the kitchen door and announced they were sending us one of their favorites. Partly out of regard for this complex genealogy, I include an article written by sister Alice describing the Alexander family tree, a brief history of the ranch itself, some lore on native game and wild foods, as well as a partial glossary of "Normanisms" — terms that were contributed originally by former chef Norman Wingate but have long since passed into the daily vocabulary of the family and the kitchen staff.

Mother, widely known as Miss Judy, passed on to us her philosophy of food, which included the appearance of the meal, the complementary tastes, the balance and nutrition, and what is appropriate to serve with what. Although my mother adopted and loved the mountain region, its people, and many of its foods, she had a unique ability to blend her elegant Virginia cuisine with the best of this region

Cataloochee Ranch

so one never knew that they were worlds apart in origin.
She also considered the entire day when she planned the
menus, which meant that if you had eggs for breakfast
you did not serve omelets for lunch, or if squash was on
the menu for dinner you did not serve pumpkin pie.
Just as bacon is good with eggs, Miss Judy believed that
certain foods go together, i.e., green beans with chicken
or pork, rice with roast beef, broccoli with lamb or beef
and so on. She balanced the dinners by making sure that
there was a meat, a starch, a green vegetable and a yellow
vegetable. The platters were always garnished for eye
appeal and refilled when empty.

    I realize that cooking has changed dramatically in the
last few years, with much more emphasis on lighter and
healthier meals. I have preserved the old-timey Cataloochee
recipes, though modern cooks can change them to suit their
needs, substituting Canola oil for bacon fat, skim milk for
whole milk or cream and Egg Beaters for whole eggs. The
easiest way to manage diets, however, is to serve yourself
smaller portions and push away from the table.

FROM TOP: *Mr. Tom and Miss Judy, 1941.*
Miss Judy, JuJu, Alice, Mr. Tom and Tom Jr., 1941.
George, 1947.

Barking Up the Family Tree

by Alice Alexander Aumen

For visitors to Cataloochee Ranch in the old days, figuring out the family tree was pretty simple — the handsome couple, Mr. Tom and Miss Judy, were the proprietors, helped along by their talented and outstanding offspring: Tommy, Juju, Atchie and Georgie.

Now, sixty or so years later, figuring out who's who gets dicey. By this time, the tree has expanded from that original stout trunk to three limbs (with grafts), six branches (with grafts) and six twigs. Add the fact that most of these appendages either live on the mountain or show up every day, and one can understand why newcomers are often cross-eyed with confusion. Herewith, Alexander Family Tree 101.

The Tom's Stand Branch: Tom Alexander, Jr., senior limb, retired, with his wife Jane Duvall Alexander (from "off") to their self-built log cabin complex at Tom's Stand. They were both accomplished journalists and editors in New York and Washington. Jane edits the Cataloochee newsletter and Tom is diverted by ski area operations and wild boar hunting, among other things.

Ames and Allison Alexander, their son and his wife, live in Charlotte, where Ames is an investigative reporter for the Charlotte Observer. Twigs are Cole and Liam.

Daughter Amanda married Steve Richards and works at the Japanese company Kyocera in nearby Mountain Home as technical marketing coordinator. Steve is with WLOS TV in Asheville.

The Coker Branch: Judy (Juju) Coker, second limb, lives in Maggie Valley, but is more frequently found either at the ranch breakfast table, the barn, rounding up renegade cattle, tending to outside lands or managing the ski area rental department. Her earliest claim to fame (at 14) was as the "youngest licensed guide in the national park system." Hers is the most prolific branch of the family tree.

Her son Richard and his wife Shelly live down Falls Road, surrounded by ranch property. Richard is a building contractor and calls a mean square dance, so he is in demand when the ranch throws a shindig. He has recently been elected President of the company, while Tom, Jr. is Chairman of the Board. Richard met Shelly when she was a wrangler at the barn. She is a ski instructor at Cataloochee Ski Area in the winter. The Coker twig is blond Melinda.

Juju's eldest daughter, Judy B., married Sammy Sutton who is head snowmaker at the ski area. Judy B. herself covers many bases — co-Barn Manager at the ranch, Bar Manager at the ski area and Olympic-caliber horsewoman. Sutton twigs are Lucinda and Matthew.

Daughter Mary, formerly Barn Manager at the ranch, is just finishing her studies in veterinary medicine at the University of Georgia. After graduation she will become a licensed veterinarian specializing in large animals, especially horses. She is also a fine horsewoman and ski instructor.

The Bear Stump Gap Branch: Alice (Atchie) married Tom Aumen (also from "off"), more frequently known as Tom John. Their 35-year career on the mountain has included ranch management, new lodge design and construction, three retail shops and ski area mountain management. Tom is now seen lovingly tending the grill at any of the three cookout locations on the property. Alice has recently resigned her position as Maggie Valley Chamber of Commerce director and plans to spend more time on the mountain.

Their son Alex currently serves as ranch General Manager while his wife, Ashli, combines duties of Business Manager for the ski area with ranch group sales and catering functions. The Aumen twig, Jorja, sprouted on August 30, 2001.

The fourth Alexander sibling, George, died of leukemia in 1955, shortly before his twelfth birthday.

The family tree is sound. While there has been some storm damage and maybe a burl or two (kinda like a wart), the Alexanders are vulnerable to only one disease, for which there is no apparent cure. The disease is known as *Mountain Fever* — its source and history have been thoroughly documented in the book of the same name. It is virulent and contagious. It incubates at an early age, relapses somewhat between adolescence and full maturity, then reappears with vigor.

A few branches show only minor symptoms, and they can live comfortably in other environs with only occasional forays back to the mountains. Others afflicted can live "off" for a few years, but are eventually compelled to return for treatment.

FROM LEFT: *Alice, Tom Jr., Miss Judy, and JuJu, 1994*

Ranger Tom Alexander on left at a cabin in Nantahala National Forest, 1926.

Barking Up the Family Tree

In The Beginning

by Judy (Juju) Alexander Coker

My father, Tom Alexander —
"Mr. Tom" as he was called, was a forester
by profession and a lover of the mountains by nature. He
was born in Decatur, Georgia, the youngest son of a respected judge. Instead of following the legal profession, he chose
to attend the University of Georgia to study forestry. While
in his early teens he spent summer months in the north
Georgia mountains with his brother, Miller, and a friend in a
foster uncle's mountain shack, fishing and hunting. The
local mountain boys took a liking to the city boys and would
collect at their shack on Sunday afternoons. It was during
these forays that Mr. Tom came to love the mountain people
and their ways. He learned how to fish and kill rattlesnakes
and how to play "Set Back" for a drink and a smell. He
learned how to hunt groundhogs and to sleep on the ground
with little or no cover. At that young age he came to admire
the humor of the sturdy mountain people, their intelligence,
clever independence and indifference to discomfort.

In the early 1920s, Mr. Tom landed a job with the
U.S. Forest Service in Franklin, NC. Eventually he went
to work for the James D. Lacey Co. in Asheville, a timber
cruising company whose job at that time was to estimate

the value of the timber and lands that were to form the Great Smoky Mountains National Park. The resulting park halted the devastating lumbering practices that were raping the entire region and, consequently, some of the beautiful virgin forests have been preserved for future generations to enjoy.

It must have been a beautiful day when Mr. Tom was introduced to the feisty, vibrant daughter of Dr. George Barksdale, an Army surgeon stationed in Asheville at the Oteen Veterans Hospital. Judith Barksdale, "Miss Judy," was born in Richmond, Virginia, and raised to city life. But summer junkets to visit country cousins taught her to know and love country life. Appropriately, she and Mr. Tom met on a trail ride. They were married in June of 1929, three months before "The Crash."

In 1930, the Lacey Company declared bankruptcy, still owing the young forester months of back wages. The only thing with which they could pay him was a stock of camping gear — tents, tables and cooking equipment — that was set up in the far reaches of the Smokies where

crews had been estimating timber for the new national park. The location of this ready-made camp in the Three Forks basin, was — and still is — one of the most isolated and inaccessible areas of the Smoky Mountains. To get there, one had to either ride or

FROM TOP: *Mr. Tom and Miss Judy on their wedding day, June 23, 1929.*
George Masa photograph of Three Forks fishing camp.

hike nine torturous miles up and down two high ridges on a barely passable trail and then travel up the rocky overgrown stream to the camp. But once there!

Picture, if you can, a magnificent, clear, trout-filled pool about fifty feet wide and a hundred feet long, fed by three brisk streams and surrounded by virgin hemlock, spruce, rhododendron, maple, beech and birch.

So without a job, a baby on the way, but with a beautiful trout stream, a national park being formed to protect it, a fully equipped camp, a cook and helper ready to work and numerous contacts in Asheville to help promote the idea, Mr. Tom and Miss Judy started the Three Forks fishing camp — their first venture into the hospitality business. They operated the camp for two summers, transporting all supplies by horse and guiding fishermen in either by foot or on horseback.

In the winter of 1932-33, the national park was in its final formative stages; the lands had been acquired and most of the inhabitants of the remote farms and settlements were being moved out. For the young ones, this represented a first glimpse of substantial amounts of green money and a first exposure to the outer world. For many, many older ones, however, it meant the loss of a home and a way of life. Those who sold their land were granted the right to remain in the park for the rest of their lives, but they had to abide by the rules of the National Park Service. That meant no hunting, no fishing out of season, no free ranging of cattle, no cutting of green wood, no loose pets and farming only in small designated areas. The settlers tried to live by these rules at first, but eventually most decided to leave their homes to make a living elsewhere.

One of the most populous and prosperous communities affected by the park's formation was Cataloochee Valley, a remote settlement near the Tennessee border. In the early 1930s

Nellie Post Office, 1933.

the valley and its suburb, Little Cataloochee, contained two post offices, three schools, three churches and about 1,200 residents. Many of the families lived in large frame houses with comfortable breezeways. Their large barns were built both for function and beauty. These self-sufficient mountain folks raised or produced most everything they needed. To buy the few things they didn't have, such as coffee and sugar, they sold apples and tobacco or drove their livestock over the mountain to the markets. Corn whiskey was a good cash crop in those days and a respected profession despite the fact that it was illegal. Some residents took in paying fishermen and tourists to add a little cash to their households. Will Hall, who owned the Preacher Hall farm at the lower end of the valley, had scooped out a three-acre lake along the banks of Cataloochee Creek using a team of mules and an old-fashioned drag. He stocked the lake with trout that he had raised in homemade pools, and he erected tent pads on the banks of Cataloochee Creek and converted a cabin or two into rooms for tourists. Any fisherman who had no luck fishing in the creek could catch trout in the lake for $.50 a fish.

During the winter of 1932-33, Chief Park Ranger John Needham spent evenings with Tom and Judy in Asheville talking about ways of attracting more tourist dollars to impoverished Western North Carolina. Needham suggested that the Alexanders lease the old Preacher Hall farm in Cataloochee Valley as a tourist destination. The couple liked the idea and named the place Cataloochee Ranch. This primitive facility without electricity, telephones, bathrooms or running water attracted guests who enjoyed trout fishing, horseback riding, Smoky Mountain pack trips and Tom and Judy's genuine warmth and hospitality. In the spring of 1935, Tom and Judy hosted the first ten-day American Forestry Association pack trip in the Smokies. Those pack trips gained nationwide attention and became so popular

The Alexanders' second foray into tourism was in Cataloochee Valley at the Preacher Hall farm.

that the Alexanders conducted them continually until 1986, except for a brief intermission during WWII.

In the valley, Miss Judy learned the self-sufficient skills of a typical mountain woman — raising young 'uns, gardening, curing meat, canning vegetables, fruits and meats, wringing chickens' necks, trimming kerosene lanterns, as well as tending to the needs of citified guests. Miss Judy also tended to the injuries and ailments of the local mountain community using tips picked up from her doctor father, who had supplied her with a well-equipped medical bag. (See page 167 for *Remedies That Work*.)

At the time, the Alexanders owned one of the few automobiles in the valley. Miss Judy used it for her weekly shopping trips over the narrow, crooked mountain road to Waynesville some 20 miles away. Going across the mountain one Saturday, she met another car that stuck to the center of the road, forcing Miss Judy off the soft right-hand shoulder. Her car rolled over six times, finally coming to rest on its side against a tree. She climbed out of the car and hiked back up to the road, hitched a ride to the ranch, borrowed a guest's car and finished her delayed shopping trip. Oh, by-the-way, she was pregnant with Sister Alice.

Though Tom and Judy had a five-year lease on the Preacher Hall farm, friction with the park service over increasingly restrictive rules and regulations forced the couple to leave Cataloochee Valley before their lease was up. But they never forgot the wonderful friends they had made there. In fact, telling and retelling funny stories and recalling ingenious pranks people played on one another filled many an evening of my childhood.

With their three children, Tom and Judy moved to Pensacola, Florida, where Mr. Tom returned to his original profession of forestry and formed his own consulting company. While cruising mahogany timber in Panama, he contracted a near-fatal case of malaria and although he recovered, he suffered periodic recurrences of fever, common to malaria victims. He soon discovered, though, that the fevers did not recur when he returned to the mountains, so he and Miss Judy began talking about how they could get back into the ranch business. Mr. Tom kept looking for the ideal location in the Smoky Mountains where they could pursue their dream. This love affair with a region is chronicled in the book *Mountain Fever*, written by Mr. Tom and finished and edited by his son Tom Jr. and daughter-in-law Jane.

He had long been aware of Fie Top, a large tract of land in Haywood County, 5,000 feet up, straddling three ridges adjacent to the Great Smoky Mountains National Park. Verlin Campbell owned the land, which had originally been cleared and farmed by the Fies and the Moodys, rugged individuals of Scotch-Irish descent. They took only what they needed from the land and gave back what they could to maintain a long-term balance. Verlin had acquired this land through inheritance, repossession on debts owed at his little store in Maggie Valley and pay-ment of property taxes for those who couldn't afford them. Eventually, however, he acquired more land than he could farm; he was "land poor."

Tom saw this property as an ideal site for a new ranch and an outlet for his enormous energy and creative imagination. The high altitude would provide cool days and nights; the rich land would be ideal for growing crops and pasturing horses, cattle and sheep; the fresh mountain springs would supply bountiful water; the woodlands would contribute plentiful timber for building and heating; and the common boundary with the National Park would offer ideal riding trails for guests. Tom and Miss Judy, with young Tommy, Juju and Atchie, spent the summer of 1938 in one of the original log cabins (still used by the ranch guests and now known as the Laurel Cabin). Tom and Verlin walked, looked and talked, and Tom knew that he had found the property he was looking for. They finally struck a deal, and Tom went into debt for the first time in his life to his mother and to one of his best friends. He purchased Fie Top in September of 1938 and work began immediately on the renovation that continued throughout the winter. By the spring of 1939, they had accomplished enough to begin taking in paying customers.

Against an architect's advice, Mr. Tom chose the large cattle barn, built mostly of mud-mortared stone, for the ranch house rather than razing it as the experts had

Converting the large cattle barn into the main lodge for the new Cataloochee Ranch.

advised. He left the existing walls, knocking holes in them for windows and doors. You can still see traces of the mud mortar today. Tom and his men sawed lumber on the place on a steam powered sawmill. He gutted the Laurel Cabin and installed a dry kiln and ran a planer with a stripped-down Model A Ford. They installed a water system using gravity feed from one of the high-altitude springs the mountain is blessed with. He built a generating system to provide homemade electricity. He did all of this during the snowy winter months.

Former "employees" of Verlin Campbell — fugitives who worked for Verlin in exchange for food and protection from North Carolina and Tennessee lawmen — did most of the work. These men felled, sawed and kiln-dried the lumber, laid the floors and built the door and window casings. They cut, split and laid the shingles for the roof. They collected rock from the fields and laid the chimney and additional walls. They installed the chestnut beams overhead in the big room and laid the buckeye logs that act as interior walls dividing the rooms.

In October of 1938, a mailing was sent to all former guests of the Cataloochee Valley resort telling them about the new place and asking for suggestions for a name. The overwhelming response was Cataloochee Ranch.

Tom Alexander always acknowledged that the heart and soul of Cataloochee Ranch was his wife, Judy Alexander, widely known throughout the mountains as "Miss Judy." While Tom was off on forestry or farm pursuits, she more or less single-handedly ran the resort, greeting guests, handling all reservations and bookkeeping, supervising kitchen and household staff, purchasing food and supplies, and, in her spare time, curing hams, raising chickens and four children, tending a large vegetable garden and simply being the best friend to children and almost everyone she knew.

Judging by her background, she was an unlikely candidate to be found working alone on a remote Appalachian mountaintop in midwinter. The daughter of Dr. George Barksdale, a well-to-do physician in Richmond, Virginia, and Mary Morton Barksdale, she was brought up in genteel fashion as a true Southern belle, complete with debutante balls, Junior League, and lessons in cooking, running a household and playing a violin.

In addition to income from paying guests, farming and other productive land uses were vital in those days, to help meet the expenses of raising four children and putting them through private schools and the colleges of their choice. Cattle grazed Hemphill Bald, sheep grazed the Sheep Pasture, and the meadows were limed, fertilized and seeded. The ranch raised its own beef, lamb, pork, dairy cattle for milk and butter along with hay to feed the cattle in winter. Like Verlin Campbell, "The Potato King," Mr. Tom raised acres of seed potatoes, rotating them each season. This kept the land fertilized and reseeded while reducing the likelihood of crop diseases. In his never-ending quest for productivity, Tom researched and tried raising all manner of crops. He dabbled in truck farming but lost patience with the tedium. He harvested timber, halted erosion, removed stumps and rocks from the pastures and even tried his hand at raising buckwheat. Many guests liked to participate in salting cattle, stacking hay or picking and stringing beans from the garden. In fact, one guest commented that he paid Mr. Tom for the privilege of working for him.

In the evenings, the long tables were laden with varieties of food, and the emphasis was on good conversation, lots of laughter and storytelling.

Almost weekly the word would go out that there was to be a square dance at the ranch and local musicians would show up to have a good time. The music was (and still is) traditional, handed down from generation to generation, learned in the home and played at any gathering. There were toe-tapping tunes to dance to, gospel tunes to sing, funning songs to laugh at and the ever-present lost-love songs. Local friends of the Alexanders were

FROM TOP: *Sheep Pasture.*
Square dance with musicians in the lodge.

welcome and came to help the city folk learn the complexities of square dancing and clogging.

Horseback riding has always been the major recreational activity. Before the National Park began restricting horses in the Smokies, pack trips were almost a weekly occurrence, ranging in length from overnight to ten days.

Mr. Tom was ever aware that the men who worked for him needed winter employment. He concocted many schemes to keep them busy in the off months, from gathering moss off logs to sell for peat to clearing new ground. One of the winter diversions Miss Judy and the ranch hands enjoyed in the forties was making their own skis. From a picture in an encyclopedia, they patterned skis out of long, thin boards, steamed them to get the ends turned up, strapped them to their feet with harness leather, and used old golf clubs for ski poles.

Original ski slope in 1961.

Whooping and hollering, they rocketed head-long off the steepest hills on the property. This gave Tom another idea that he wrestled with for years. In 1959, he and Miss Judy made a winter tour of the New England states, coming as far south as Virginia's Homestead, then the nation's southernmost ski resort. In 1961, Cataloochee opened the first ski area in North Carolina on the little hill behind the ranch house and many of Tom's mountain friends finally had all the winter work they could use.

Mr. Tom lived to see the ski area moved to the north side of Moody Top before he died in 1972. Miss Judy continued to welcome guests with that special smile of hers until 1997, when she died quietly at home with her children around her. At her funeral, Reverend David Reeves, in describing what an exceptional person Miss Judy was, said the Alexanders came to the region, bought the mountain, but didn't change it.

The eldest child of Tom and Miss Judy, Tom Jr., spent his working years writing for *Fortune* magazine, retiring to Fie Top where he and his wife, Jane, built an authentic mountain log home with exquisite attention

Lunch atop Charlie's Bunion on the Appalachian Trail in the Great Smoky Mountains National Park

to interior décor and simple natural landscaping. He is responsible for protecting our lovely Hemphill Bald by placing it in a conservation easement administered by the Southern Appalachian Highlands Conservancy, a private organization dedicated to the preservation of the world's oldest mountains. And just this year, thanks to the help of good friends who live on Fie Top, we placed the Moody pastures in a similar easement.

Alice and her husband, Tom John Aumen, spent many years as managers of the Ranch until their son, Alex, was old enough to take the reins. Now they enjoy traveling, pursue civic activities and advise and help at the Ranch. While Tom John and Alice were in the management position, they recognized that our guests' expectations were changing and that we needed to devote more attention to maintenance, lawn and garden care and hospitality accents. Gone were the days when the horses grazed the front lawn and around the cabins. The meadow was no longer cut for hay; so that beautiful area is now reserved for the horses and cattle to roam at will. This is a good change. The animals now have their freedom and space when they are not working and the guests don't need to walk through "stuff" to get to dinner.

I was actively involved in the day-to-day kitchen and staff management until the third generation was old enough to take over. Now I care for the ranch outer lands, fencing and trail maintenance and do volunteer trail maintenance for the Great Smoky Mountains National Park, especially the section of the Appalachian Trail that runs through the park. I am also president of CRT, Inc., the company that runs the riding stables for the Ranch.

My son, Richard, was just recently elected president of the company, while brother Tom is Chairman of the Board. My daughter, Judy B., manages the barn, replacing daughter Mary, who left to enter vet school.

I get many questions on how the ranch has changed over the years. While we all miss the magnetism and charm of Miss Judy and Mr. Tom, the family has made a point of keeping up with the times while retaining the heritage and history we are so proud of. The ranch has grown larger, but its soul is still the same.

We've added recreational facilities, and we see that grounds are carefully manicured. We have built four popular new cabins for a total of 11 family cabins. We have expanded and refined our food service to meet the more demanding needs of the public. High-altitude farming is no longer profitable so our only agrarian effort now is grazing cattle to keep the high meadows open and maintaining a barn full of trail horses.

Today there is more emphasis on activities for children and grownups alike. One of the favorite things for children to do is to find the swamp monster's house down by the lake and let their imaginations go to work. Evening entertainment is geared to all ages. Freeman Owle, a favorite, tells Cherokee stories around the fire. Mark Hufford, a wildlife rehabilitator, tells stories about the animals he has rescued. Rob Gudger and his gray timber wolves visit us regularly. There are magic shows, sing-alongs, mountain music, square dances, moonlight hikes, wagon rides, hot dog and marshmallow roasts and wine tasting parties. But the best entertainment of all is to find a place to sit after riding across Hemphill Bald and watch the cattle graze up on the meadow while the clouds drift lazily overhead.

Some things never change. We still ring the same old bell, an antique A Model brake drum, that called people to all meals in Cataloochee Valley. We continue to sit at long tables, giving guests a chance to strike up new friendships (This works so well that several groups of guests who cemented friendships at the ranch return at set times every year). Instead of place cards, we still use clothespins

Stopping for a sip of water at a ford at Caldwell Fork.

In The Beginning   23

with names inked on them just as Miss Judy did. Family members often join guests at meals. Regulars are Alice and Tom John who, on cookout nights, are invaluable help to Patsy at the grill. I enjoy breakfast and the early morning scene.

We are lucky to have a core staff of loyal mountain neighbors who have been with us for years. Cordelia (Cookie) Fisher first came to work for Miss Judy as a teenager in the mid 1940s. With a few years off to raise a family and get them through school, she has been with us ever since. Cookie's dedication to her job and her very pleasant personality are reasons I like to be at the breakfast table. I know she will make sure everything is just right.

Cookie's son, Jerry, is maintenance supervisor and, like all the mountain people, can do anything — electrical work, plumbing and handle our complicated water system to insure we don't run out of water during dry times. With his able staff, he manicures the grounds so they look like a picture from a gardening catalogue. If cattle get out, he knows the way to get them back in. If a tree falls across a trail, Jerry and his boys cut it and split the wood for the fireplace.

The backbone of the kitchen is the Woody family. Patsy Gaddis, who came to Cataloochee when she was 17, is now head chef and doer of all things. Her brother, Tommy Dale Woody, is breakfast and lunch cook and their mother, Thelma (Granny), is the dishwasher. I seldom hear any of them complain that they work too hard, that we give them too much to do, or that we have too many special things going on at once, though all of the above are true at times. If there is no one to pick vegetables from the garden, they do it. If we are out of the homemade jams and jellies, Patsy makes more, even though the house is full of people who insist on eating three meals a day. This sort of dedication to the job and the ranch gives us owners a comfort zone comparable to a leisure chair.

Here I am climbing Rendezvous Rock at age 8.
I think I've always been adventurous.

Normanisms

People in the ranch kitchen find it hard to cook without the unique vocabulary contributed by former chef Norman Wingate. Norman came from Asheville, North Carolina, in the early 1950s to start cooking for Miss Judy and remained with us until his retirement in the mid-1970s. A fine, if somewhat temperamental, cook he had his own terms for most situations, terms that are still in use at the Ranch.

For instance, whenever you need to bake bread or a cake you must *free heat* your oven. Spicy dishes taste better with a dash of *tobacco sauce*. Whenever we want to know what supplies are on hand, we go to *interview* the freezer, the storeroom or the garden, and around the kitchen you use a *repairing* knife to peel vegetables. Sometimes, you *spearmint* on a new recipe, but you always have to keep in mind that if you mix lemon juice and milk together they will *yodel*.

Of course, not all was work with Norman. When he felt talkative, he enjoyed a *colitical discussion*, especially with someone so educated that *the ABCs ran out of his nose*.

FROM LEFT: *Mr. Tom, Norman and a ranch hand frying up a batch of trout.*

Many times Norman would get into a rather unpleasant mood and, knowing that the meal would suffer, Miss Judy would engage him in conversation of any sort to lighten the atmosphere. At this time Norman would say, *Miss Judy, you'se practicin' psychology on me*.

He also liked to go to Asheville on his day off, but had a habit of spending all his money immediately and then calling Miss Judy to ask her to wire him more. After awhile, Norman himself became so embarrassed over this habit that one day he told Miss Judy: *If the phone rings, and it's Norman, don't answer it*.

He was very sensitive, and if he felt that someone had been unkind to him, they had *hurt his dignus*. Also, when the ranch was full and the dining space limited, we might have to set a table on the *balconette*.

But probably the most often used Normanism is the one for events that happened long before you or I can remember, i.e., *many B.C.s ago*. Now that's a long time.

Norman died in 1999 after a brief illness, but will long be remembered not only for his cooking abilities but also for his fine sense of what is proper and what is not.

Breakfast & Brunch

Breakfast & Brunch

FROM TOP: *Grinding cane for molasses, Cataloochee, 1936, The Plateau Studio, Asheville, N.C. Clingman's Dome from Raven Knob.*

iss Judy believed that every meal
should be special, particularly breakfast. The unique way in which she
combined things of the city where
she was born with things of her new
country lifestyle led to a beautiful blend of the two. When
the Alexanders moved to North Carolina the mountains
were populated with the descendants of the Scotch-Irish
who settled Western North Carolina and Eastern Tennessee.
These hardy folk were accustomed to hard work, hard living,
belly-filling food and plenty of fun in their spare time. Food
was taken seriously not only as a filler but as a symbol of the
generosity and interdependence of life here. In an argument
one man could be heard to say to another, "I thought I could
trust you. You ate at my table." Perhaps though preparing a
meal was warm like a quilt, the center and backbone of the
home where mouthwatering smells filled the house.

In those days the mountain family in the cabin would
arise about 5:00 a.m., the men to chop the kindling and
start the morning fires while the women fetched the water
from the spring to start the coffee brewing. Breakfast was not
a light meal. While it was in the making, the men would
start feeding the livestock and gathering the tools for the
day's work. When the men came in for breakfast about 6:00
a.m. the table groaned with sliced salt pork, sausage, biscuits
and gravy, eggs, grits, pork chops, chicken, creamed corn or

baked apples. Homemade butter, jam or sorghum molasses were always on the table along with milk and coffee.

Miss Judy very gracefully melded the Virginia breakfasts she was raised on with what she learned from her mountain neighbors. From Virginia she served fruits and juices, hot cereals, sometimes spoon bread and fried green tomatoes; from the mountains she included gravy, biscuits, country ham, trout and potato cakes. She also added hot cakes, French toast and her specialty, Cataloochee Puffed Toast. This toast is in reality a fritter, using slices of bread coated in a thick batter and deep fried. Delicious served with syrup or honey.

Though hardly traditional, brunch is a nice way to entertain at mid-day by serving a combination of breakfast and luncheon dishes: omelets, cheese grits, bacon, sausage, chicken livers, fried green tomatoes and of course bloody Marys, screwdrivers and mimosas.

Cataloochee Puffed Toast or Pain Perdue (Lost Bread)

This is a favorite and makes a great brunch item for special guests. Maybe the whole family is special on Sunday morning. Slice 12 pieces of bread on the diagonal. It works best if you cut the slices of bread the night before and leave them out in the air overnight. This recipe will serve about 8, and you can figure about 1½ diagonal slices per person. Make the following batter.

2	cups plain flour	½	tsp. nutmeg
4	tsp. baking powder	1	egg
	(Rumford is best)	1	tsp. vanilla
½	cup sugar	1½	cups milk
½	tsp. salt	2	Tbsp. shortening
1	tsp. cinnamon		

Mix dry ingredients, then mix in liquids. The batter should be quite thick. Coat each slice of bread liberally. Drop into about two inches of hot (375°F) shortening. Turn when the underside is brown. Brown both sides and drain on paper towel. To serve, dust the toast with powdered sugar and put syrup and honey on the table.

Fried Apples

6   tart apples   3   Tbsp. bacon drippings
    (Granny Smith's are fine)   ½   cup sugar

Leave the skins on the apples, and slice and core them. Heat the bacon drippings in an iron skillet. Add the apples. Sprinkle with sugar. When almost tender, turn and cook a little longer. Drain and serve with scrambled eggs, bacon, grits and biscuits. Serves 6.

Tommy Dale's Apple Stuffed Toast

Tommy Dale Woody, the brother of head chef Patsy Gaddis, first came to work for us as a dishwasher and never missed a day of work or came in a grouchy mood. It didn't take long for him to move up to breakfast and lunch cook and both meals are always interesting when he's on duty.

2   cups applesauce   1   tsp. cinnamon
    or apple butter   ½   tsp. nutmeg
½   cup sugar   12   slices of bread, sliced thick

Mix the first four ingredients. Spread on the bread and make a sandwich. Butter each side of the sandwiches and place on a greased hot grill. Brown on both sides then slice them diagonally and serve sprinkled with powdered sugar. Serves 6.

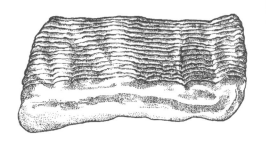

Oven-Fried Bacon

Place bacon strips on a cookie sheet so that they do not overlap each other and bake at 350°F until crisp, about 10 minutes. Place on paper towel to drain. Save the bacon drippings for other uses.

Sautéed Chicken Livers

Chicken livers are delicious accompanied by bacon or dished up over rice or toast points. They are a wonderful brunch item.

2	lbs. chicken livers, (cut into bite-sized pieces)	1	cup flour
			salt and pepper to taste
1	medium onion, diced	4	Tbsp. bacon drippings

Dredge the livers in flour seasoned with salt and pepper. Place in a hot skillet with the bacon drippings. Add the onions and fry quickly on both sides, drain on a paper towel. Omit the onions if you prefer. Serves 6.

Blueberry Muffins

¼	cup shortening	2	cups self-rising flour
½	cup sugar	⅔	cup milk
2	eggs	⅔	cup blueberries (fresh, canned or frozen)

Cream shortening and sugar. Beat and add the eggs. Sift flour and add alternately with the milk. Keep about ⅓ cup flour to coat the blueberries. Stir floured berries in lightly. Spoon into greased muffin tins and bake at 400°F for 30 minutes. Makes 12 muffins.

Buckwheat Cakes

Looking for a way to use some of his unproductive land, Mr. Tom had the idea of growing buckwheat. He hoped to raise a tasty crop and, at the same time, attract grouse and quail to his lands. He chose the backside of Run Around Hill, which is in the middle of Windy Gap. The spot was unsuitable for hay and most other crops because of its steepness.

It wasn't long until he realized that he had taken on a tough project. The men had to plow the ground with a team of horses, then plant the grain by hand. They harvested the buckwheat with old-fashioned mowing scythes and finally had to beat the grain from the stalks with canes and toss it into the air to winnow out the chaff. Nor was it simple to find a mill that would grind the grain, since buckwheat darkens the millstones. After the job was done, the miller had to clean the stones thoroughly by grinding "waste" corn. Mr. Tom finally conceded that he had produced the most expensive buckwheat flour in the world, but that it sure made delicious pancakes. These days you can buy buckwheat flour in specialty stores and, it too, makes mighty fine cakes!

1	cup buckwheat flour	2	Tbsp. shortening
1	cup self-rising flour	2	cups milk
1	egg		

Mix all ingredients together and spoon onto a greased griddle (The griddle is hot enough when a small amount of water spatters on it). Turn the cakes when bubbles start to form. Serve piping hot with homemade fruit syrup (see page 37), New England maple syrup or honey. Serves 6.

French Toast

Tommy Dale came up with this version of French toast. The addition of flour to the traditional way of fixing French toast keeps the bread from being soggy and gives better texture.

10	slices of thick-sliced bread	¼	cup sugar
1	cup flour	2	tsp. cinnamon
1½	cups milk	1	tsp. nutmeg
1	egg	2	tsp. vanilla

Mix the milk, eggs, sugar and spices. Drop the bread slices into the mixture, coating them well. Then drop onto a hot greased griddle and brown on both sides. Before serving, slice the bread diagonally and sprinkle with powdered sugar. Serves 8.

Homemade Hot Cakes

To this basic mixture you can add blueberries, apples, strawberries or whatever pleases you.

1	cup self-rising flour	1	Tbsp. syrup or sugar
1	egg	1	Tbsp. shortening
1	cup milk		

Mix all ingredients together thoroughly. "Free heat" your griddle. It is hot enough when a drop of water spatters when dropped on it. Spoon the mixture on, letting it drop off the end of the spoon to keep the cakes round. Turn when bubbles start to appear on the top. Serve immediately with homemade fruit syrup, maple syrup or honey. Serves 4.

Fruit Syrups

These syrups are good on morning hot cakes and French toast. They are also tasty on ice cream. The best way to get your fruit juice is to place the fruit in just enough water to cover and boil about 10 minutes. Drain. When peeling peaches, save the peelings and pits and boil them. The peach flavor is much more distinct. Discard the fruit. If you mash the fruit, you may get the pulp into the juice and it won't be clear.

1	cup fruit juice	1	Tbsp. cornstarch
1	cup sugar		water

Cook the fruit juice with the sugar about 5 minutes. Thicken with the cornstarch dissolved in a small amount of cold water. Simmer 10 minutes. You can use any fruits for this: blackberry, blueberry, peach, strawberry, elderberry, etc.

Toasted Biscuits

When leftover biscuits are toasted, the flavor and texture change entirely. They are delicious and always get gobbled up.

See Breads for biscuit recipe. Slice leftover biscuits, dot with butter and brown under the broiler. Good with homemade elderberry jelly.

Corn Cakes

There are so many things you can do with cornmeal that no one ever tires of. My grandmother served spoon bread for breakfast (see breads and cereals), but we usually use it for dinner. Cornmeal mush is an item the older people cooked for breakfast and served with plenty of homemade butter. We use cornmeal for breading fish, squash, tomatoes, okra, poke salad, etc.

1	cup Three Rivers Corn Meal Mix		
¼	cup self-rising flour	1½	cups milk
1	egg	1	Tbsp. shortening

Mix all ingredients together. Spoon onto hot greased griddle and turn when bubbles start to form. Serves 4.

Cornmeal Mush

1	cup Three Rivers Corn Meal Mix	salt to taste
2	cups water	

Mix the all ingredients and cook on medium heat, stirring often. Mush is done when it is good and thick. Have plenty of butter on hand. Serves 4.

Oatmeal

1	cup Quaker Oats Oatmeal	2	cups cold water
	(not instant)	½	tsp. salt

Put the oatmeal into the cold water and add the salt. Bring to a boil, reduce heat and simmer for about 5 minutes, stirring occasionally.
If you put the ingredients into a double boiler, you don't have to stir while you are cooking the rest of the breakfast. Serves 4.

Grits

Many people from the North cannot understand our love affair with grits and often find them bland and uninteresting. The taste for grits does have to be acquired, but true Southerners will hotly defend them and pity the poor soul who tries to tell a grits lover how to eat them. Grits are usually served for breakfast, but are good for brunch or supper eaten with country ham and red-eye gravy or fried trout.

Grits are coarser ground than cornmeal. They are made from corn that has had the hull removed from the kernel by soaking it in lye. Then it is washed and washed and finally ground. You can now buy quick grits that are quite good and easier to cook than the old-fashioned kind.

1   cup Quaker quick grits
4   cups water (or 2 cups water and 2 cups milk)
     salt to taste

Put the grits and salt into the water and bring to a boil. Reduce to simmer and cook about 10 minutes, stirring often. Serve with lots of butter. Leftover grits can be smoothed into a square pan and refrigerated for fried grits later on. Serves 8.

Cheese Grits

While you are cooking the grits, add some grated cheese of your choice. Sharp cheddar or Parmesan are good choices.

Fried Grits

Remove the congealed leftover grits from the pan and slice into serving slices. Dip into a beaten egg. Place in a skillet or on a hot grill coated with a little shortening or bacon drippings. Fry until brown on both sides.

Potato Cakes

Leftover potatoes are good for breakfast or supper.

1½ cups mashed potatoes
½ cup flour
1 egg

⅓ cup onion, minced
salt and pepper to taste
4 Tbsp. bacon drippings

Combine first four ingredients and spoon onto a hot skillet with bacon drippings. Fry until brown on both sides. Serves 6.

Hash Brown Potatoes

4 leftover baked potatoes
2 Tbsp. bacon drippings

1 Tbsp. butter
salt to taste

Dice the leftover potatoes and place in a pan with the bacon drippings and butter. Fry until brown. Serves 4.

Sawmill Gravy

Sawmill gravy was actually a main staple of the backcountry logging camps. Those hard-working men needed a substantial breakfast, and the camp cook saw that they got it. The breakfast would include country-fried steak, hot biscuits, pork side meat, sausage, gravy and eggs.

2 cooked sausage patties
4 Tbsp. sausage drippings

½ cup flour
2 cups milk
salt and pepper

Put the sausage drippings in a skillet and stir in the flour. Cook on medium heat, stirring occasionally until light brown. If you want a white gravy, don't brown the flour. If you want a darker gravy, let it brown more but don't burn it. Add the milk and cook until thick, stirring occasionally. Crumble the sausage patties into the gravy and season. Add milk if too thick. Good on anything; biscuits, grits, eggs, potatoes, cornbread, etc.

Soups

Soups

FROM TOP: *Cataloochee Ranch snow scene.*
Mr. Tom in the potato field.

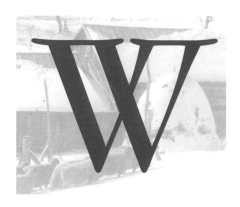

hoever invented soups must have a special place in that "Great Kitchen" in the sky. What to do with leftovers? Make a soup. What to fix for a light Sunday night supper? Soup and an open-faced sandwich. What to do for a sick one in bed with a cold? Mother's chicken soup, of course. It is a great way to use your imagination in the kitchen.

Over the years each of our chefs has made a favorite soup — the one that they prepared best. Miss Judy's favorite was turkey noodle soup, which she would vary by substituting rice instead of noodles or adding corn, and or both. Our present chef, Patsy, makes a killer cabbage soup that is gobbled up by folks who would ordinarily never touch cabbage. The irascible Norman would clean out the entire refrigerator and make an irresistible vegetable soup. When Jessie Jenkins cooked for us in the 1970s he made a wonderful cream of broccoli soup, using our fresh garden broccoli and a cheese of his choice. Cookie Wood, though never a ranch chef, provided his delicious potato soup recipe. Brother Tom brought his Senate bean soup down from Washington, DC, and it fits in beautifully with Cataloochee cooking.

Cream of Asparagus Soup

As my mother always said, don't throw away anything that you might be able to use later. In this case it is the bottom ends of the asparagus that you should save. When cooking asparagus, bend the stalk and it will snap where the tender part starts. Put these ends into a quart of water with a little salt and boil vigorously for about 15 or 20 minutes. Finally you can discard those ends. There! You have your stock for the following recipe!

1	quart asparagus stock	1	celery stalk, diced
1	quart chicken stock	1	stick butter
1	bunch of asparagus tips	4	Tbsp. flour
1	small onion, diced	1	cup half and half
1	carrot, diced		salt to taste

    Chop the asparagus tips fine, but save a few for garnish on top of the soup. Sauté the finely diced onion, carrot and celery in the butter about 5 minutes. Stir in the flour to make a roux then add the two stocks and the asparagus tips. Simmer awhile before adding the half and half. Simmer a little longer to blend all the flavors. Check for seasoning and serve with the asparagus garnish. Serves 6.

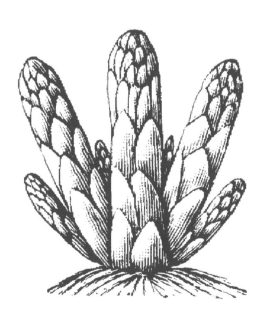

Black Bean Soup

A delicious soup that can be prepared in a jiffy.

Sauté together in olive oil
1   red onion, chopped   1   clove garlic, minced

Add
4   16-oz. cans of black beans   1   tsp. cumin
   salt and pepper   2   dashes of balsamic vinegar
2   4-oz. cans of green chilies   16 oz. beef stock or bouillon
1   Tbsp. thyme   16 oz. medium salsa

    Simmer about 10 minutes to blend all flavors. Serve with a dollop of sour cream. Serves 12.

Senate Bean Soup

    Brother Tom Alexander brought this recipe down from his working days in Washington, but it translates beautifully to the mountains with its beans, ham, sausage and potatoes. He also donated the recipe for Ramp Soup, which I have listed under the section on Wild Game and Food from the Woods.

1   lb. dry navy beans   1   cup onion, chopped
1   ham hock   ¼   cup parsley, chopped
   (smoked sausage is also good)   1   tsp. thyme
1   gallon water   2   bay leaves
1   lb. potatoes, peeled and cooked   ¼   cup milk
1½ cups celery, chopped   1   clove garlic, chopped
                                     salt and pepper to taste

    Soak beans overnight or cook soup an extra half-hour or so and add extra water. Boil beans, ham, spices and garlic 1½ hours or until beans become fairly tender. Mash the potatoes and blend with milk and salt and add to the beans. Add celery, onions and parsley. Simmer 1 hour. Crush a cup or two of the beans and return to the soup to thicken. Remove ham and chop fine and return to the soup. Check for seasoning. Serves 12.

Cream of Broccoli Soup

1	quart broccoli, left-over, chopped or 1 bunch cooked, chopped	1	medium onion, chopped
1	can whole kernel corn	2	celery stalks, chopped

Boil all the above ingredients in about 1 gallon of chicken stock.

1	can evaporated milk	salt and pepper to taste
½	cup shredded cheddar cheese	

Mix these last ingredients and stir into the soup mixture. Simmer and stir until you reach the desired thickness. Serves about 12.

Country Cabbage Soup

1	lbs. ground beef	1	small head cabbage, shredded
1	medium onion, diced	½	gallon water
1	medium green pepper, diced	1	Tbsp. oregano
3	celery stalks, diced	2	tsp. salt
1	28-oz. can diced tomatoes	1	tsp. black pepper

Combine first 4 ingredients and cook until vegetables are done. Drain well. Add remaining ingredients. Simmer for 45 minutes to 1 hour. Serves 8.

Jane's Cream of Celery Soup

Sister-in-law Jane Alexander is a true artist when it comes to soups.

4   Tbsp. butter, divided
1   clove garlic, minced
1   cup onion, coarsely chopped
¼   cup flour
4   cups root or knob celery, cubed,
       about 1½ pounds

8   cups rib celery, trimmed,
       cut into one-inch lengths
4   cups chicken broth
4   cups water
    salt and pepper to taste
½   cup heavy cream

Sauté onion and garlic in 2 Tbsp. butter. Sprinkle with flour and stir to blend. Add celeries, chicken broth, water and salt. Bring to a boil and simmer for 45 minutes. Puree in a food processor or blender and return to kettle. Add cream, salt and pepper to taste. Swirl in remaining 2 Tbsp. butter. Serves 8.

Tom John's Cataloochee Ranchili
(actual title at the Chili Challenge — "My Own Damn Chili")

This recipe was recently prepared by brother-in-law Tom John Aumen for the President's Day Chili Challenge, held in Maggie Valley every February. He came off with First Place in the Best-in-Restaurant Division and also Best Overall. He did add the ramps, so maybe that's what got him the honors.

2   lbs. ground round or chuck
1   large onion, chopped
1   green bell pepper, diced
2   16-oz. cans kidney or pinto beans
2   16-oz. cans diced tomatoes
2   16-oz. cans tomato sauce
1   4-oz. can chopped green chilies

2   cloves garlic, minced
3   Tbsp. chili powder
2   tsp. cumin
1   Tbsp. cider vinegar
2   Tbsp. sugar
    salt and pepper to taste
½   cup ramps, chopped with
       greens (if you have them)

Brown ground beef with the onion and green peppers in large iron skillet. Drain fat if necessary. Add garlic, canned ingredients (do not drain) and the other seasonings. Simmer at least one hour without covering, adding liquid if you prefer. Better the next day and just fine for freezing. Serves 8.

Fish Chowder

2	bacon slices, diced	2	cups half + half or milk
1	medium onion, diced	½	stick butter
1	lb. white fish		salt and pepper
2	potatoes, diced	1	gallon fish stock
		1	cup flour

To make the fish stock

Place the fish into 1 gallon of salted water and bring to a boil. Cook about 8 minutes. Remove the fish and strain the liquid. Let the fish cool then remove all bones.

Sauté bacon until crisp. Sauté onion in drippings. Stir in flour to make a roux. Add fish, potatoes, salt, pepper and fish stock. Simmer until potatoes are tender (about 30 minutes). Add the half + half and butter and bring to a boil. Serve piping hot. Serves 12.

Gazpacho

This is a marvelous summer soup traditionally served cold. Vegetables are fresh and abundant, and you can use whatever you have on hand. The vegetables listed below are just suggestions.

2	tomatoes, peeled, seeded and quartered		fresh basil leaves, chopped
1	green pepper, cored, seeded and quartered	3	fresh cilantro leaves, chopped
1	onion, peeled and quartered	⅓	cups tomato or V-8 juice
1	large clove garlic, minced	¼	cup red wine or balsamic vinegar
1	cucumber, peeled and cubed		cup extra virgin olive oil
2	cans green chilies, chopped		Tabasco to taste
			salt and pepper to taste

Put all ingredients in blender or food processor and liquefy. Serve with garlic croutons. Serves 4.

Jane's Mushroom Soup

2 lbs. mushrooms
   (I like to mix shitake, oyster
   and baby bellas with regular
   mushrooms.)
4 Tbsp. butter

salt and pepper to taste
2 cups beef broth
1 cup heavy cream
1 cup freshly chopped onion
¼ cup flour

Sauté mushrooms and onions. Sprinkle with flour, salt and pepper. Simmer in beef broth for 15 minutes. Puree in food processor or blender. Return to the heat and bring to a boil. Add cream. Can be served hot or cold. Serves 4.

Cream of Tomato Soup

1 small onion, diced
1 small green pepper, diced
3 Tbsp. flour
6 Tbsp. butter

2 cups milk
1 large can tomato juice
1 small can stewed tomatoes
   salt and pepper to taste

Sauté the onion and the pepper in the butter until the onion is transparent. Stir in the flour. Gradually stir in the milk, tomato juice and stewed tomatoes. Check for seasoning. Simmer and serve. Serves 6.

Cookie's Potato Soup

Cookie Wood got his name because his mother wanted a girl. Aletha Wood preferred helping her husband with the farm-work to cooking for the family of four boys, so she taught Cookie a lot of the mountain ways of cooking, including this recipe for "tater" soup. Other things in which he became proficient were banjo pickin', farming, excavating and just about anything else that is worth doing.

6	potatoes, peeled and sliced	1	onion, diced
1	gal. water	1	28-oz. can diced tomatoes
	salt and pepper to taste	1	28-oz. can whole kernel corn

Boil potatoes in salted water until almost done. Add onion and continue boiling. Cook this until it comes all to pieces. Add the tomatoes and the corn. If further thickening is desired, stir in about 2 Tbsp. flour mixed with cold milk. Check the seasoning. Serves 10.

Miss Judy's Vegetable Soup

1   gallon water
1-2 soup bones or leftover beef
    salt and pepper to taste
1   24-oz. can tomato juice
1   onion, diced
3   celery stalks, diced
4   carrots, diced
½   cup ketchup

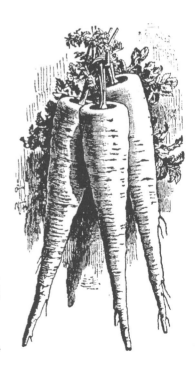

Cook soup bones in salted water until tender and save the stock. Cut the meat from the beef bones and add to the stock along with any fresh or leftover vegetables,such as beans, corn, potatoes. Add tomato juice, ketchup, onion and celery. Salt and pepper to taste. Simmer about 1 hour to blend all the flavors. Serves 12.

Miss Judy's Turkey Soup

First the bird and then the soup! Miss Judy would never waste a thing, and so she taught us to do the same. Not only is it economical, but the flavors are better.

1	turkey carcass	1	medium onion, diced
	water	2	celery stalks, diced
	salt and pepper	1	clove garlic, minced
6	Tbsp. butter	2-3	cubes chicken bouillon
4	Tbsp. flour	1	cup milk

Cut off all the usable slices left from a roast turkey, wrap them and save for later use. Boil the carcass in enough salted water to cover for about 30 minutes. Strain off the stock and set aside. When the carcass is cool enough, pick all meat from the bones and chop into bite-sized pieces. For 1 gallon of soup, melt the butter in a large pot. Sauté the onion, garlic and celery about 4 minutes. Make a roux by adding the flour and stirring. Using a wire whip, gradually add the stock, stirring constantly. Dissolve the chicken bouillon in small amount of hot water and add to the soup. Add the chopped turkey and milk. Check for seasoning. To give more body, use either 2 cups cooked noodles, leftover cooked rice and/or 2 cans whole kernel corn. Let simmer until all flavors are blended. Serves 12.

Posole

A favorite of Tom Alexander's — serve with garnishes to make a meal.

2 ancho chilies
2 pasilla chilies
  (or substitute hot dried chilies)
1½ lbs. boneless pork loin,
  cut into one-inch cubes
2 chicken breasts,
  cut into bite-sized pieces

2 quarts water or chicken broth
1 onion, chopped
1 tsp. dried thyme
2 garlic cloves, crushed
1 Tbsp. vegetable oil
1 bay leaf
2 16-oz. cans whole hominy

Place chilies in a bowl and cover with water. Soak for several hours.

Put pork in a kettle and cover with broth. Add the onion and one clove of garlic, bay leaf, thyme and salt to taste. Bring to a boil and simmer, skimming the surface to remove scum and foam. Cook for 15 minutes, then add chicken. Cook for additional 15 minutes.

Drain the chilies, remove the stems and seeds. Put into saucepan with 1½ cups water. Bring to a boil and cook until tender. Pour into food processor with remaining clove of garlic and blend to a fine puree. Heat the oil in a saucepan and add the puree, stirring. Add salt to taste. Rinse out the processor with a little water and add to saucepan.

Drain one can of hominy and add to kettle. Pour second can with its liquid into kettle. Continue cooking for 30 minutes, skimming scum and fat.

Serve in hot bowls. Put garnishes in serving bowls to be passed at table. Garnish with toasted tortillas or corn chips, shredded lettuce, thinly sliced radishes, crushed oregano leaves, cayenne pepper, lime wedges, freshly chopped cilantro or avocado peeled and cubed.

Meats

Meats

FROM TOP: *Miss Judy and Molly Ordway in the Sheep Pasture, 1940.*
Cows in the pasture.

As in most fine restaurants, meats play a starring role at Cataloochee Ranch. Meats range from country to what Norman would call "real up town" and this variety keeps our guests' palates fresh. Foods indigenous to the South — ham, fish and fried chicken are on the menu regularly but beef of all sorts, lamb, pork and Cornish game hens are also included.

As a child I remember the days before freezers and relatively little refrigeration. Foods were preserved either by canning, drying or storing in a root cellar. Early winter was the time to kill the hogs that had been fattening in the pen all summer. This was an opportunity for "a working" with neighbors helping out and getting "paid" with sections of meat. All hands set about scraping the hair off the hog, skinning, rendering the lard and making cracklins for cornbread. At hog-killing time Mother had lots of help and the women ground the sausage, then seasoned, fried and canned it. They stored the jars upside down to let the fat settle to the top so that when the jar was opened, the fat was on the bottom. They laid hams on tables in the storeroom and salted them down, the first step in curing. Later Mother would wash and recoat the hams with a sugar mixture to cure for the rest of the winter. Finally she sacked them in the spring for long-term storage.

The storeroom where we kept the hams had a screen window to allow plenty of air circulation. One spring day assistant cook and dishwasher, Fred, was sitting beside the building, stringing beans and trying to get rid of a hangover headache. Hearing some noise, he looked up to see a large bear exiting the storeroom through the back window with a prize ham in his mouth. You can imagine the image of Fred running to the kitchen door, almost white with fright and stammering, "Miss Judy, the bear got the ham. The bear got the ham." The men organized a bear hunt, the bear was killed thus providing more meat for canning. Oh so good.

Beef Bourguignon

Sister-in-law Jane notes that this rich winter classic takes a little time to prepare but always gets an enthusiastic reception. It can be made a day or two ahead, leaving you free for other chores the day of the dinner party. It is good left over and freezes well. If you end up with extra gravy, you can turn it into a great soup by adding water, beef, vegetables, rice or whatever.

8 oz. thick-sliced bacon,
    cooked and crumbled
    Reserve two Tbsp. drippings
4 lbs. beef chuck,
    cut into one-inch cubes
1 cup onions, chopped
3 Tbsp. flour
3 cups good Burgundy
    (Ask your wine merchant.
    Serve the same burgundy
    with dinner.)

3 cups good beef broth
2 Tbsp. tomato paste
1 Tbsp. fresh rosemary, chopped
4 carrots, peeled and sliced
2 cups pearl onions,
    cooked according to package
2 lbs. mushrooms,
    preferably wild ones
1 Tbsp. butter
1 Tbsp. currant jelly
    parsley, chopped for garnish

Preheat oven to 350°F. In a Dutch oven, brown beef in bacon drippings, a few pieces at a time. Add onions and sauté. Sprinkle with salt, pepper and flour. Cook for five minutes. Add wine, stock, tomato paste, bacon and rosemary. Bring to a boil, cover and bake in oven for 2 hours.

Meanwhile prepare the vegetables. Boil carrots until tender about five minutes. Drain. Sauté sliced mushrooms for 10 minutes. Cook pearl onions. Remove casserole from oven and transfer to a burner. Add carrots, onions, mushrooms and currant jelly.

Heat through and serve with chopped parsley. Serves 8 to 10.

Ground Beef Casserole

Served with tossed salad and corn on the cob, this casserole makes a nice light supper or hearty lunch.

1	lb. ground beef	4	Tbsp. flour
1	small onion, diced	1	cup water
	salt and pepper	2	cups noodles, cooked
1	garlic clove, crushed	½	cup cheddar cheese (optional)

Place first 4 ingredients in a skillet and brown. Stir in flour, then add water and stir over medium heat until thick. Check the seasoning. Into a casserole put a layer of the meat mixture, then a layer of the noodles, another layer of meat and noodles, and finish with the meat mixture. Top with a little cheddar cheese if desired and bake at 325°F until bubbly. Serves 4.

Roast Beef au Jus

Serve with these tasty dishes — Rice, Fresh Garden Broccoli, Onion Casserole, Homemade Rolls and Chocolate Soufflé with real Whipped Cream.

1   standing rib roast, 7 to 8 lbs. (3 or 4 ribs)
    salt and pepper

Rub the roast with salt and pepper. Place in a roasting pan with the fat side up using the ribs as a rack. Pour in about 1 inch of water and roast at 425°F for 30 minutes. Reduce the heat to 350°F and continue roasting another 1½ hours. Allow about 15 minutes per pound for medium rare beef. Save all the drippings for the au jus. Let the roast stand and "rest" about 15 minutes before carving. Slice across the grain. Serves 8.

Beef Stroganoff

This is a wonderful way to use leftover roast beef.

2	lbs. beef	6	oz. mushrooms, sliced
	flour with salt and pepper	6	oz. white wine
4	Tbsp. butter	½	tsp. nutmeg
1	medium onion, sliced	4	Tbsp. sour cream
1	clove garlic, minced	16	oz. beef stock

You can use either leftover beef roast or fresh beef. Cut the beef into 2-inch strips and dredge in the seasoned flour. Brown the meat quickly in the butter adding more butter if needed. Then place the meat into a large pot. Meanwhile sauté the onion and mushrooms in a little butter and add to the meat mixture. Add the beef stock to almost cover the meat and begin simmering. Stir to keep from sticking. As this simmers, add the white wine and the nutmeg. The stroganoff will thicken as it simmers. Taste for seasoning. Just before serving, stir in the sour cream and serve in the middle of a noodle ring garnished with fresh parsley. Serves 4.

Pepper Steak

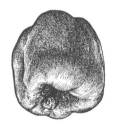

2	round steaks,
	cut into 1-inch strips
1	medium onion, sliced
1	green pepper, sliced
4	Tbsp. butter
4	Tbsp. flour
1	cup beef bouillon
	salt and pepper to taste

Sauté the onion and green pepper in butter and set aside. Season the flour well with salt and pepper and dredge the steaks, then brown them in the butter on both sides. You may need to add more butter if the pan is dry. Stir the flour into the butter and add the bouillon, stirring until the desired gravy thickness is reached. Place the meat in a roasting pan, pour in the gravy, top with the onion and pepper and cover tightly. Bake at 325°F until tender, about 45 minutes. This goes well with Easy Rice (see page 99). Serves 4.

Sautéed Sirloin Tips

When trimming any steak, save the ends and cut into bite size.

1	lb. sirloin tips		salt and pepper to taste
1	onion, sliced, rings separated	1	clove garlic, minced
1	green pepper, cut into strips	4	Tbsp. butter

Melt the butter in a skillet. Put in all the items and sauté about 5 minutes, stirring. Add salt, pepper and minced garlic. Serve over cooked noodles or rice. Serves 4.

Pot Roast of Beef

Liberally sprinkle a bottom round roast with salt, pepper and minced garlic. Pour in 1 can of condensed mushroom soup and 1 packet of onion soup mix. Cover tightly with aluminum foil and bake at 325°F for 1½ hours or until tender. To serve, thicken the drippings slightly with a flour and water paste and dribble over the sliced beef.

For a variation on this pot roast, place the roast seasoned with salt and pepper in a Crock-Pot, pour in 1 can of condensed vegetable soup. Turn the pot on low for 6 to 8 hours. The whole house smells delicious when you come home from work.

Bobbie Toole's Beef Stew

Bobbie and Demi Toole have a charming house on the mountain and Bobbie spends a lot of time here while Demi comes whenever he can break loose from his cardiology practice. When he was a child, Demi's parents brought the entire family for weeklong stays. Bobbie served this stew one fun-filled night at their house and I knew that it had to be included in the cookbook. So good and different!

2	lbs. lean stew beef	2	Tbsp. olive oil
¼	cup vermouth	2	onions, sliced
2	Tbsp. gin		

Marinate the stew meat in the mixture above in a plastic bag in the refrigerator 1 hour or overnight.

1	onion, chopped	1½	cup chicken broth (to cover)
1	cup celery, chopped		salt and pepper to taste
¼	tsp. thyme	2	carrots, sliced diagonally
1	clove garlic, crushed	½	cup green beans, blanched
1	cup crushed tomatoes	¼	cup peas
1	cup white wine	¼	cup corn

optional: ½ cup sautéed mushrooms
½ cup pearl onions, peeled and blanched

Drain and discard the marinade. Pat meat dry and brown in 1 to 2 Tbsp. oil. Discard the remaining oil. Deglaze pan with wine, add meat and cover with chicken broth. Add chopped onion, celery, garlic, tomatoes and thyme. Simmer 1 hour. Heat oven to 325°F and bake in covered casserole 1 hour. Drain, saving juices. Add 2 Tbsp flour to thicken. Season with salt and pepper. Mix all and return to oven for 30 minutes. Serve with wide noodles or rice.

To shorten time, simmer 30 minutes, bake 30 minutes, thicken, add vegetables and bake covered 30 minutes.

Beef Stew

1	lb. stew meat	2	onions, diced
3	carrots, cut into bite-sized pieces		salt and pepper to taste
3	potatoes, cut into bite-sized pieces	4	Tbsp. flour
2	celery stalks, chopped	1	dash of Kitchen Bouquet

Simmer meat in enough salted water to cover for about 30 minutes. Add the vegetables and continue simmering another 30 minutes. Make a paste with the flour and a little water and stir in. Add a dash of Kitchen Bouquet to the desired darkness and check seasoning. Simmer another 5 minutes, stirring, and serve. Serves 4.

Meat Loaf

1	lb. ground chuck	1	cup uncooked oatmeal
1	small onion, diced	1	egg
½	green pepper, diced	½	cup ketchup
1	clove garlic, minced		salt and pepper to taste

Combine all ingredients, mix well using your hands and mold into the shape of a loaf pan then place in the pan. Bake at 350°F about 1 hour. Saltine crackers may be substituted for the oatmeal for a change in flavor. Serves 4.

Mushroom & Tomato Gravy
(to go with the Meat Loaf)

¼	cup meat loaf drippings or butter	6	oz. sautéed mushrooms
¼	cup flour	2	cups tomatoes, diced, fresh or canned

Brown the flour in the drippings and stir in the tomatoes and the mushrooms. Cook until thick, stirring constantly. Check for seasoning.

Chicken & Dumplings

Remove any giblets that may be in the cavity of a 4- or 5-pound whole chicken and set them aside for other uses. Place the chicken in enough salted water to cover it and simmer about 45 minutes. (You can set a crock pot on low, add the chicken, salt and water to cover and forget it for 3 hours.) Remove the chicken and set aside to cool.

Dumplings

You can make the following dumplings or you can buy very nice ones in the store in the frozen bread section. You may also use canned biscuits broken into small pieces if you like a lot of bread in your dumplings.

2	cups plain flour	1	egg
1	tsp. salt	1	cup chicken broth

Mix flour and salt, stir in beaten egg and add stock. Roll out onto floured board and cut into thin strips. Drop strips into simmering stock. Cook 20 minutes at medium heat. While the dumplings are cooking remove the chicken from the bone and break into bite-sized pieces. Add the chicken to the dumplings and stock and check for seasoning. If you prefer a little thicker mixture use 3 Tbsp. flour mixed with 4 Tbsp. water and stir into the chicken. Serves 8.

Oven-Fried Chicken

Not as good as traditional fried chicken, but very tasty and much better for you. To accompany the chicken, I recommend Mashed Potatoes with Giblet Gravy (see below), Fresh Green Beans, Sliced and Buttered Beets, Hot Biscuits and a Fruit Cobbler.

Dredge 1 cut-up fryer in a mixture of flour, salt, pepper and paprika. Spray a cookie sheet with cooking spray and place the chicken on it. Then spray the chicken. Bake at 350°F until golden brown about 1 hour. No need to turn. Serves 4 or 5.

Chicken Giblet Gravy

While the chicken is frying in the oven, place the neck, liver, heart, gizzard and 1 egg in about 2 cups of water. Add a little salt and simmer about 10 minutes. Remove the meat from the neck and gizzard and dice the liver. Chop the egg. Collect the drippings from the fried chicken in a separate pan and add 2 Tbsp. of flour, stirring to make a roux. Gradually add the stock, stirring until smooth and the right thickness. Taste for seasoning. Add the giblets and chopped egg for an elegant southern gravy.

Chicken with Broccoli or Snow Peas

6	chicken breasts, boned and skinless salted and peppered	½ cup celery, diced quite fine
½	cup white wine	½ cup onion, diced quite fine
½	cup fresh mushrooms, sliced	1 cup broccoli or snow peas, cooked

Brown the chicken breasts on both sides, then reduce the heat and fry until done. Set aside. Sauté the mushrooms, celery and onion in the white wine until the onion is transparent. Stir in the broccoli or snow peas. When serving, place the vegetables on top of the chicken. Makes a pretty platter.

Bettina's Fish Cakes

Bettina and George Shackelford, who winter in West Columbia, Texas, spend summers in a log cabin built by Mr. Tom in Still Hollow, site of a notorious mountain still. George, an artist, paints portraits and landscapes, makes wooden bowls, lamps and sculptures (some from tortuous rhododendron roots), and has lately taken to sculpting busts. Bettina is a great cook who likes to innovate.

1 lb. cooked trout or other fish, deboned	½ cup mayonnaise
juice of 1 lime	2 large eggs, beaten
2 Tbsp. chives	½ cup red pepper, finely chopped
2 tsp. basil	½ tsp. red Tabasco or 1 tsp. green Tabasco
4 tsp. shallots or green onions, finely chopped	1½ tsp. Dijon mustard
½ cup good tartar sauce	4-6 cups fresh bread crumbs

All ingredients must be finely chopped. Mix everything but the fish together. Now add the fish and smush with your hands. Make cakes and dust lightly with flour. Fry lightly, just enough to get good and hot. These can be made ahead and frozen.

Rainbow Trout

Serve the trout with Spoon Bread, Fresh Green Beans, then pick out a yellow vegetable like Stewed Squash, add Homemade Biscuits and you have a tasty and well-balanced meal.

I hope that you have caught your own fish so you know they are fresh. Fish about 8 inches long are fine for frying whole, but any bigger than that and you would want to fillet them. Clean the fish, removing the heads if you want to. Traditionally trout are served with the head intact, but some people object to this. Dredge the fish in well-salted and peppered cornmeal. Fry on medium heat in a goodly amount of bacon drippings or vegetable oil until well browned on both sides. Drain on paper towels.

Baked Country Ham

My grandmother always kept a cooked country ham in her refrigerator, for she never knew when company was coming, and a Southern hostess always had something on hand to feed them. In those days, friends and relatives visited a lot, often without notice, and thought nothing of staying a week or two. To go with her country ham, she always had the makings for Spoon Bread, Red-Eye Gravy and plenty of Biscuits. She kept lots of butter and an abundance of fresh vegetables for her table. We children were taught that we didn't have to put everything on our plate, but what we did take we had to finish or "make a soldier's plate."

Wash and scrub a country ham to remove all mold. Soak overnight in a mixture of 1 cup vinegar, 1 tsp. baking soda and enough water to cover. Next morning, boil the ham in fresh water for three hours or until the hock bone pops out. Remove and trim off all excess fat. Score and coat with brown sugar and sprinkle with ground cloves or stick with whole cloves. Place in a roaster, add about ½ inch of water and bake at 350°F about 30 minutes. Let cool at least 30 minutes before carving.

Red-Eye Gravy

This gravy is delicious on grits, potatoes and hot biscuits.

Into the drippings in the roaster, add ½ cup strong coffee and a little more brown sugar. Skim off excess fat. If you wish to have a little thicker gravy, stir in a small amount of flour mixed with water and bring to a boil.

Roast Leg o' Lamb

When Miss Judy served her Roast Leg o' Lamb dinner with Uncle Ben's Wild Rice Mixture, Fresh Garden Broccoli, Onion Casserole, Homemade Yeast Rolls and Strawberry Mousse. Norman would say, "Miss Judy, that dinner's way uptown."

Generously sprinkle the leg of lamb with salt, pepper and minced garlic on both sides. Place in a roaster with slices of onion, a stalk of celery and a carrot. Pour in about 1½ inches of water and roast in a  350°F oven about 2 hours. Remove to cool on a carving board and strain the drippings into a pot for gravy. When cool, slice across the grain and serve garnished with wild mint.

Gravy for the Leg o' Lamb

Refrigerate the drippings from the lamb so that the fat will rise and congeal. Skim. Heat the drippings. Make a paste with 3 Tbsp. flour and a small amount of cold water. Stir into the gravy pot and add 1 cup of white wine. Bring to a boil and stir until smooth and season with salt and pepper to taste. A teaspoon of mint jelly adds interest to this gravy.

Lamb Curry

2	lbs. lamb stew meat or leftover leg of lamb cut into bite-sized pieces	1	carrot, peeled and diced
		4	Tbsp. butter
		4	Tbsp. flour
1	onion, diced	2	tsp. curry powder
1	celery stalk, diced		salt and pepper to taste

Boil the lamb in salted water until tender. Save the stock. Sauté the onion, carrot and celery in the butter, then add the flour and simmer until the roux is brown. Add the stock, lamb, salt, pepper and curry powder. Taste for seasoning. Serve over a bed of rice with assorted condiments such as grated coconut, peach chutney, diced hard-boiled eggs, finely chopped onions, chopped nuts and raisins or currants soaked in brandy.

Jane's Easy Lasagna

The secret to this easy lasagna is layering pasta, meat sauces and cheeses without first cooking the pasta.

1	box lasagna noodles	2	cloves garlic, minced and sautéed
1	large can spaghetti sauce		
1	lb. hamburger meat, cooked, drained and crumbled	2	onions, finely chopped and sautéed
1	lb. Italian sausage, cooked and thinly sliced	2	cans green chilies, diced
1	tsp. thyme	3	cups mozzarella cheese, grated
1	tsp. oregano	3	cups ricotta cheese
1	dash of nutmeg	3	cups Parmesan cheese, grated

Put canned spaghetti sauce in saucepan. Add thyme, oregano, nutmeg, minced garlic, sautéed onions, diced green chiles, 1 lb. cooked ground meat drained of grease and 1 lb. Italian cooked sausage. Simmer for 45 minutes. Place 2 cups of sauce in bottom of 13 x 9 inch pan. Add layer of uncooked lasagna noodles. Follow with more sauce and then a layer of cheeses. Repeat with another layer of each until ingredients are all gone. Save enough mozzarella and Parmesan to completely cover top. Bake at 350°F for 45 minutes. Allow to rest. Serves 8 to 10.

Place leftovers in individual freezer bags and freeze. To reheat, defrost, remove from bag and bake covered with aluminum foil at 350°F for 20 minutes.

Marinated Pork Loin

Sister-in-law Jane swears by this recipe, which is easy to prepare, very tasty and low in calories. It always gets good reviews.

1   pork tenderloin, split in half

Marinate tenderloin with soy sauce, sherry, garlic, salt, pepper and ginger root for 8 to 10 hours in a glass or ceramic oven-proof pan. Reserve marinade. Preheat oven to 325°F. Lower heat to 140°F and put tenderloin in the oven. Cook for 1½ hours or until meat thermometer shows medium. Add pan juices to the marinade. Cook over medium flame until reduced to a nice au jus consistency. Slice pork thinly and serve accompanied by the gravy. Serves 6.

Baked Pork Chops

A good accompaniment to pork chops is potatoes of any kind, Fresh Garden Greens, Scalloped Tomatoes, Biscuits and, of course, a delicious Dessert.

Dredge chops in flour seasoned with salt, pepper and paprika. Brown the chops in a frying pan in a little olive oil or on the grill. Then place them in a roaster that contains a rack, pour in a cup of water, cover with foil and bake at 325°F about 1 hour.

Cornmeal Gravy
(to go with the pork chops)

½   cup bacon drippings   2   cups milk
½   cup cornmeal   salt and pepper to taste

An iron skillet makes the best gravy. Place the bacon drippings in a skillet, add the cornmeal and cook on medium heat, stirring frequently, until light brown. Add the milk and the salt and pepper and stir. If too thick, add a little more milk.

Turkey with Dressing

Turkey is one of the most versatile of all meats. Here are just a few ideas.

Sprinkle a 12- to 14-lb. turkey liberally with salt and pepper inside and out and dot with butter. Place the bird in a roaster containing a rack and pour in about 4 cups water to help with the gravy and the dressing. Cover loosely with foil and bake at 350°F about 2 hours or until the meat thermometer reads 175°F. Remove the foil for the last 30 minutes so that the turkey can brown nicely. Let the bird cool about 15 minutes before carving. Save all the liquid to use in the dressing and the gravy. A 10-lb. turkey feeds about 10.

For the gravy, follow the recipe for Chicken Giblet Gravy, using the turkey stock for your liquid. While the turkey is baking, simmer the giblets in salted water to make more stock. If you have any stock left over, put it in the freezer.

Leftover slices are tasty in Turkey Divan. The slices can be wrapped and frozen, but don't keep them in the freezer too long. Save the turkey carcass for soup.

Cornbread Dressing

4	cups cornbread, crumbled	½ cup butter for sautéing
1	cup leftover wheat bread, crumbled (optional)	2 eggs
1	onion, diced	4 Tbsp. rubbed sage
3	celery stalks, diced	salt and pepper to taste
		2 cups turkey stock or broth

Make a pan of cornbread according to the instructions on the bag and add any left over bread that you might have. Sauté the onion and the celery. Crumble the cornbread and the other bread into a mixing bowl and add all the other ingredients. Pour in the turkey stock, enough to make the mixture almost soupy. Taste the dressing to make sure the seasoning is correct. Bake at 350°F about 35 to 40 minutes. This will make about 10 servings.

Baked Oyster Dressing

2	doz. oysters and liquor	½	tsp. cayenne pepper
2	Tbsp. vegetable oil	3	bay leaves
2	cups onions, chopped	1	tsp. garlic, chopped
¼	cup green onions, chopped	¼	cup parsley, chopped
1	cup bell pepper, chopped	1	cup water
1	cup celery, chopped	4	cups white bread, cubed
1½	tsp. salt	½	cup Parmesan, grated

Sauté onion and garlic in oil about 5 minutes. Add and sauté green onions, bell peppers and celery. Mix in water, oyster liquor and bread. Cook 2 to 3 minutes stirring constantly. Remove from heat. In

 mixing bowl combine bread mixture with oysters, cheese, bay leaves, salt, cayenne and parsley. Mix thoroughly. Butter 9 x 11 inch baking dish and pour in mixture. Bake at 325°F for 1 hour or until bubbly and golden. Remove bay leaves. Serve hot. Makes 5 cups.

Turkey Divan

4	Tbsp. butter	1	bunch of broccoli,
4	Tbsp. flour		slightly cooked and cut into
½	cup white wine		serving-sized pieces
1½	cups milk		turkey slices
			optional: cheese, grated

Melt the butter and stir in the flour and cook for about 2 minutes. Gradually stir in the milk, then the wine. Cook and stir about 2 minutes. Salt and pepper to taste. Into a quart casserole, place slices of turkey or chicken. Put in a layer of the broccoli. Then add another layer of the meat slices and a little more broccoli. Pour the white sauce over all of this and bake at 325°F until bubbly. Shred some cheese on top if you like. Serves 4.

Miss Ducky's Turkey Hash

Jane Alexander writes: "For as long as I've known him, my husband Tom has bragged about his grandmother's delicious turkey hash, a favorite for breakfast waffles or Sunday suppers. Hoping to recreate this acclaimed dish, we conferred with Miss Judy before her 89th birthday and came up with a version we think will please. Miss Judy learned to cook from her sweet-tempered mother, Mary Morton Barksdale, nicknamed 'Miss Ducky,' in an un-PC age because of the way she walked."

4 Tbsp. butter or turkey pan drippings	1 cup cooked turkey, cut into bite-sized pieces
4 Tbsp. flour	1 dash of nutmeg
2 cups milk	2 dashes of Tabasco
1 parsley sprig, chopped dash or two of good sherry	2 dashes of Worcestershire salt and pepper to taste

Combine the milk with parsley. Melt the butter or pan drippings and, using a wire whisk, stir in the flour and cook to make a roux. Gradually pour the milk into the butter-flour mixture, stirring constantly. When the mixture is thickened and smooth, simmer gently for 5 minutes, stirring occasionally. If the sauce seems too thick, add a little more milk. Add the seasonings, cut-up turkey and any leftover turkey gravy to the sauce and heat. Stir in sherry just before serving. Serve over waffles, flaky biscuits or English muffins.

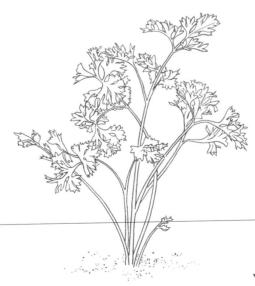

Stuffed Peppers

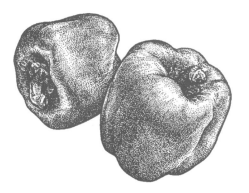

4 medium green peppers,
    seeded, and divided in half
2 Tbsp. butter
1 medium onion, diced
1 lb. ground beef
2 cups cooked rice
    salt and pepper to taste

Sauté onion lightly in the butter. Combine ½ the onion, meat, rice, salt and pepper. Stuff into the hollowed-out peppers and place in shallow pan. Pour in 1 inch of water. Cover the peppers with the following sauce:

½ the sautéed onion   1 can stewed tomatoes
1 small can tomato sauce

Combine all ingredients, spread over the peppers and bake at 350°F for 30 minutes.

Vegetables

Vegetables

FROM TOP: *A photograph of the ranch on which Mr. Tom penciled in the masterplan. Trail ride circling around the garden with The Balsam Mountains in the distance.*

hen Mr. Tom was making plans for Fie Top in 1938, he took a photograph of the ranch layout and penciled in the location of buildings, pastures and even a ski slope.

On this photo he also drew in a place for the ranch garden. When it came time, he carefully fenced an acre and terraced it so that drenching rains would not wash away the precious topsoil. He made sure that the exposure was to the Southwest to make the best use of the sun. Over the years we have moved the garden to other places hoping to leave the weeds behind, but we've finally come to the conclusion that you cannot leave weeds behind. Besides, if weeds grow well, then the soil and conditions must be good for vegetables. So we have returned to the original plot.

Beginning about the first of July, we start harvesting vegetables that grace the tables. Cool weather plants do the best: broccoli, cabbage, Brussels sprouts, lettuce, beans, cucumbers, squash, beets, kale, mustard and our very favorites, snow peas and sugar snap peas. Corn, tomatoes, okra and eggplant prefer warmer climes, so we rely on local farms at lower elevations to furnish these.

The land up here is so rich and productive that tales have been written to boast of what it can grow.

My Dad loved to josh with his mountain neighbors about who employed the most ingenious farming methods and who could raise the largest vegetables.

Dad told the story of Uncle John, who lived on a plot of land as steep as a mule's face. Uncle John claimed that the ground's steepness was actually an advantage. He said he planted his potatoes in rows running up and down the hill. Then to dig them in the fall, he merely had to open the bottom of the row and the potatoes would all run into the sack he held. He said his only problem arose one day when his son made the mistake of opening the row without getting the bag into position quick enough. All the spuds rolled down the mountain to the creek and thence to the river, headed for the ocean.

Whereupon Uncle John reasoned, "Well, Tom Alexander's always braggin' about his taters. I'll just go borry a half-bushel from him."

So up the mountain he went, carrying his half-bushel basket to where Tom and his crew were digging potatoes.

"Say, Tom, looks like you've got a fair crop of taters this year. I'm needin' just a half-bushel of little 'uns for the missus to bile up. Reckon I could get some from you?"

"Well," Tom drawled, "I'd sure like to oblige you, Uncle John, but I just can't see fit to cut one of my taters in half. Oh, by the way, my corn's getting ready to cut. Reckon you could bring that cross cut saw back you borried?"

"Yeah, Tom. I sure will bring it back just as soon as some of the young'uns can hep me get it out of a cucumber that it got hung in."

GREEN VEGETABLES

Fresh Asparagus

We've never grown asparagus, but Miss Judy always wanted to and I plan to one day.

Look for small, bright green stems, as they are the most tender. Use as soon as you can, and if you must keep them overnight, place in a dampened brown paper bag in the refrigerator. There is no need to cut off the tough ends. Just bend each stalk and it will break where the stem starts to get tough. Try it, it works! Save the ends for soup.

1	bunch fresh asparagus	1	egg, hard-boiled, and diced
	salt to taste	2	Tbsp. olive oil or butter

Break asparagus as described. If you have a steamer, that is great, but if you do not, you can use a pot with just enough water in it to barely cover. Steam or boil about 4 minutes so that the asparagus remains slightly crunchy. Remove to a warm platter and drizzle with the olive oil or butter and sprinkle with salt. Scatter the egg over the top. Serves 4.

Green Bean Casserole

1 quart leftover green beans
8 oz. sour cream
1 cup fresh mushrooms, slightly sautéed in butter
  almond slivers

This is a delicious way to prepare leftover green beans. Combine the first three ingredients and put them in a 1-quart casserole dish. Top with the almonds and bake at 325°F until hot. Serves 4 or 5.

Cornfield and Half-Runner Beans

They are called Cornfield Beans because they grow quite tall and need something to climb on so, rather than using another piece of ground and putting stakes in the ground, the old farmers killed two birds with one stone. They planted the beans when they planted the corn and as the corn grew up it gave the beans something to wrap around. The pods are long with large beans in them and are very easy to string and snap. Their flavor is so good. I like to select beans that have a lot of mature and yellowing pods in them so that I can shell out some of the beans to mix in with the green ones. Half-Runner Beans are so called because they also like to climb but not quite so far. Their flavor is delicious.

    2   lbs. beans
    3   slices of salt pork
    ½   tsp. sugar
        salt to taste

String and snap the beans and wash thoroughly. Place in a pot with just enough water to cover, add salt pork, salt and sugar. Bring to a boil then reduce to a simmer and cook about 45 minutes. Add water if the beans are getting too dry, but most of the water should be boiled out when done. They are done when quite tender. Taste for seasoning. Serves 6.

Beans and Corn

Cook fresh beans as described above until almost done. Add the corn cut from four ears and a little more salt. Cook about 10 minutes.

Broccoli

After the first large head of broccoli is gathered don't think that is the last of it. Each plant will keep producing small heads around the original stem that are just as good or even better than the first one. You can gather broccoli until frost. Just spray for the cabbage looper worm. Our garden produces beautiful broccoli and plenty of it! Gather the heads before they start to flower.

1   head of fresh garden broccoli, cut into serving-sized pieces
    water to cover
1   tsp. salt

Wash thoroughly. Bring the salt and water to a boil and toss in the broccoli. Bring it back to a boil and cook about 3 minutes, uncovered. Drain and serve with melted butter. (If you cannot get garden fresh broccoli, you will need to cook it a little longer.) Serves 5.

Broccoli-Corn Bake

1   cup fresh corn cut off the cob or 1 16-oz. can of whole kernel corn
1   bunch of steamed broccoli, cut into serving-sized pieces
1   egg, beaten
1   cup saltine cracker crumbs   4   Tbsp. butter, melted
1   small onion, diced   salt and pepper to taste

Sauté the onion in ½ the butter then combine corn, broccoli, onion, egg, ½ cup cracker crumbs, salt and pepper. Turn into 1-quart casserole. Combine the remaining cracker crumbs with the remaining butter and sprinkle over the vegetable mixture. Bake in 325°F oven for 25 to 30 minutes. Serves 6.

Cassoulet

Jane says this French country dish from Gascony is a great crowd pleaser. She often brings it to hiking retreats, where it easily feeds 14 to 20 after making judicious additions of meats and beans. Can be prepared ahead and is good left over or frozen.

2 lbs. dried white beans,
   soaked overnight
   (Great Northern or
   flageolets if available.)
1 5-lb. turkey
2½ lbs. lamb stew meat
2 lbs. boneless pork shoulder,
   cut into bite-sized cubes
1 lb. thick-sliced bacon,
   cooked and crumbled
   (Reserve drippings.)
2 Tbsp. dried thyme
1 tsp. allspice

2 Tbsp. olive oil
   bacon drippings
2 cups onions, chopped
4 large carrots,
   peeled and chopped
2 cups good dry white wine
1 6-oz. can tomato paste
4 cups good beef stock
5 bay leaves
10 garlic cloves, minced
1½ lbs. kielbasa sausage
   fresh parsley
   fresh bread crumbs

Preheat oven to 400°F. Drain the beans and place them in large flameproof casserole with a lid. Cover with water and bring to a boil. Reduce heat and cook briskly uncovered for 15 minutes. Remove from heat and let stand in cooking liquid.

Remove giblets from turkey. Set aside. Salt and pepper turkey inside and out and roast in oven for about 2 hours. Turkey will be underdone.

Brown lamb cubes in skillet on the stove. Remove to a bowl. Sauté the pork and the reserved giblets in same skillet. Remove to bowl with lamb.

Sauté onions and carrots in same skillet until tender, adding bacon grease as needed. Remove to bowl. Transfer contents of bowl with a slotted spoon to the pot of beans, which have been soaking in their liquid.

Add liquid from bowl along with wine to the skillet and bring to a boil. Lower the heat and cook briskly until the wine has reduced slightly and all browned particles have dissolved 5 minutes or so. Pour into beans.

Stir tomato paste, beef stock, reserved juices, thyme, allspice and bay leaves to beans. Add minced garlic and additional water if needed so liquid just covers beans. Cover the casserole. Bake 2 hours or so.

Remove, uncover, and cool to room temperature, stirring occasionally. Cover and refrigerate. Refrigerate cooked turkey.

Next day, prick garlic sausage and simmer in water for 30 minutes. Drain and reserve.

Skin the turkey and pull meat from bones and cut into chunks. Stir into the beans.

Sprinkle bread crumbs and parsley over the beans. Bake for 1½ hours. Serve hot from the oven. Serves 12.

Cabbage Creole

Zucchini, lima beans or eggplant can be substituted.

1   head of cabbage,
      cut up but not too fine
1   onion, diced
2   celery stalks, diced
1   green pepper, diced
1   28-oz. can diced tomatoes

1   tsp. sugar
3   Tbsp. butter
½   cup ketchup
      salt and pepper to taste
1   Tbsp. garlic, minced

Sauté onion, pepper, and celery in butter until onion is transparent. Add tomatoes, cabbage, sugar, salt, pepper, garlic and ketchup. Simmer about 15 minutes. Serves 6.

Steamed Cabbage

1   head cabbage, chopped
1   tsp. sugar

      salt to taste
4   Tbsp. butter

Plunge the cabbage into just enough salted boiling water to barely cover it. Add the sugar. Cook about 10 minutes. Drain and season with the butter.

Stuffed Cabbage

1	small head cabbage	1	lb. ground beef
1	medium onion, diced		salt and pepper to taste

Remove the outer leaves of the cabbage and plunge into boiling water for a few seconds to wilt them. Chop the remaining cabbage, but not too fine. Combine meat, onion, cabbage, salt and pepper in a skillet and sauté for 5 minutes. Place the meat mixture in the wilted cabbage leaves, roll and secure with a toothpick. Place them in a pan and cover with the following sauce:

1	small can tomato sauce	salt and pepper
1	can stewed tomatoes	

Bake at 350°F for 30 minutes. Serves 6.

Fresh Garden Greens

Kale, mustard, collards or a mixture of all are particularly good with pork or fish. Greens shrink a lot when cooked so you will need what looks like twice as much as you would think.

Wash the greens thoroughly and twist them into small pieces. Bring a pot of salted water to a boil and toss in the greens. Add about 3 slices of salted pork. Boil 15 minutes and check seasoning. Cook them until they are tender, then drain and serve. Serve with a cruet of vinegar on the table.

Steamed Snow Peas

Snow peas are the original Chinese variety and can be found in most supermarkets, but are quite expensive. Sugar Snap peas are a fine substitute. You would cook them the same way, allowing just a little more cooking time.

String and snap 2 lbs. snow peas. Drop the peas into rapidly boiling salted water, add a touch of sugar and bring again to a boil, then turn off the heat. Drain and season with a generous amount of butter. If you use sugar snap peas, they need to boil about 2 minutes.

YELLOW VEGETABLES

Candy Roaster Puff

A candy roaster is a member of the pumpkin family, but has a much more delicate flavor and does not have the stringy texture. It is indigenous to these mountains and comes in all colors, shapes and sizes from ugly warty green to a gorgeous orange hue, from quite small to huge. In this area, the County Fair has competitions for the largest candy roaster and last year one weighing 450 pounds walked off with the blue ribbon. The owners treat them like babies to achieve their goal, placing the young squash on a clean bed of hay and religiously picking off any competing siblings so that their prize will get all the nourishment from the parent plant. They water at precise times in precise amounts and appoint guards at night to watch for vandals.

Cut into chunks, it freezes very well without blanching. If you can't get a candy roaster, you may use sweet potato or butternut squash. If you have taken a candy roaster home with you from the mountains, here is a hint on peeling it. It has a very tough outer skin and is very hard to cut and peel, so saw it in half, scoop out the seeds and place it in a 325°F oven for about 30 minutes. Then you can scoop out the pulp and freeze it as is or make the following puff.

2 cups cooked candy roaster, mashed with a little butter. (If you are using raw chunks, place them in a small amount of water and simmer about 15 minutes or until very tender and mushy.)	⅓ cup sugar pinch of salt 2 eggs 1½ cups milk ½ tsp. vanilla 1 tsp. cinnamon ½ tsp. nutmeg

Mix all ingredients together and turn into a buttered 1-quart casserole. Bake at 325°F until set, approximately 45 minutes. Serves 5 or 6.

Corn on the Cob

6   ears of fresh corn
    salt to taste
    butter, melted to spread on the corn

Shuck and silk the corn using a small scrub brush to get all the silk. Place into a pot of boiling salted water and bring to a boil. Allow to boil about 2 minutes. Remove, drain and serve with the butter. Serves 4.

Corn Pudding

A good use for leftover corn. Just cut the kernels off the cobs.

2   cups whole kernel corn   1   tsp. sugar
2   cups milk   salt and pepper to taste
2   eggs   paprika

Beat the eggs and milk together. Add corn and the seasonings. Pour into a greased 1-quart casserole, top with a little paprika and bake at 325°F for 1 hour.

Creamed Corn

Another use for leftover corn on the cob. This recipe calls for you to twice-cut the corn. That means that you slice the tips off the kernels and then scrape the knife blade down the cob in order to scrape out the milk of the corn.

2   cups corn, twice cut   1   cup milk
    salt and pepper to taste   2   Tbsp. corn starch
1   tsp. sugar

Mix all ingredients together and bring to a boil. Stir and simmer about 5 minutes.

Succotash

Mix cooked corn, cooked lima beans and 2 Tbsp. of butter and heat. For added interest, pour in a can of stewed tomatoes, heat and serve. Check for seasoning.

Fried Eggplant

Use this batter for squash, cucumbers, cauliflower and even fish fillets.

Make a batter with

1 cup self-rising flour	1 cup milk
1 egg	1 tsp. garlic, minced

Peel and slice eggplant into ½ inch slices. Salt lightly. Dip into the prepared batter and fry quickly in 2 inches of vegetable oil until brown on both sides. Drain on paper towels and sprinkle with salt.

Macaroni and Cheese

2 cups macaroni, cooked	1 cup milk
1 cup good sharp cheddar cheese, shredded	1 egg
	salt to taste

Place alternate layers of macaroni and cheese in a buttered quart casserole, reserving 4 Tbsp. of the cheese for the top. Beat the egg and the milk and salt and pour over the macaroni. Sprinkle the remaining cheese on the top and bake at 325°F until set, about 45 minutes. Serves 4 or 5.

Miss Judy's Onion Casserole

This recipe has been used at the ranch for as long as I can remember, so I suppose that Miss Judy originated it. I also have never seen it in any other cookbook. It is so simple and so good and is probably the most request-ed of all recipes, except possibly the Candy Roaster Puff.

3 medium onions	12 oz. good sharp cheddar, grated
1 12-oz. can evaporated milk	salt to taste

Chop onions into spoon size pieces and boil in salted water until transparent, about 5 minutes. Drain and place half the onions in a greased 1-quart casserole. Put in a layer of cheese, then the rest of the onions then the rest of the cheese. Pour in the milk until it barely covers the onions. Bake in a 325°F oven until bubbly and the cheese is melted, about 30 minutes. Serves 4 or 5.

Okra and Tomatoes

½ cup onion, diced
½ cup carrot, diced
½ cup celery, diced

2 cups small okra pods
2 16-oz. cans diced tomatoes
salt and pepper to taste
olive oil

Sauté onions, carrots and celery in a small amount of olive oil about 3 minutes. Add tomatoes and okra and bring to a boil. Simmer about 3 minutes and serve. Serves 6.

Baked Acorn Squash

You may also use butternut squash.

2 acorn squash
2 Tbsp. butter

½ cup brown sugar
1 tsp. cinnamon

Cut the squash into quarters and scoop out the seeds. Combine all the other ingredients and spread into the cavity. Bake at 325°F about 30 minutes. Serves 8.

Squash Casserole

2 cups yellow or zucchini squash or both, cooked
2 cups milk
2 eggs
4 Tbsp. butter

1 onion, diced
2 cloves of garlic, minced
salt and pepper to taste
dash of paprika (if desired)

Sauté onion and garlic in butter. Beat eggs and milk together. Add the squash and salt and pepper and mix well. Pour into a quart casserole and top with a little of the paprika. Bake at 325°F for 45 minutes.

Try mixing broccoli and cauliflower into this basic recipe and you would have a mélange. One thing you should not do is add beets. I tried it and the result was disastrous. The flavor was okay, but the appearance was not. Serves 5.

Squash Fried in Meal

Slice yellow squash. Roll in cornmeal seasoned with salt and pepper. Fry in a pan that has about 4 Tbsp. bacon drippings or vegetable oil in it. Fry, turning often until golden brown. Use this same method for okra.

Stewed Squash

6   medium yellow squash
       or 3 yellow and 3 zucchini,
       cut into bite-sized pieces
1   medium onion,
       cut into bite-sized pieces
     salt and pepper
2   Tbsp. butter

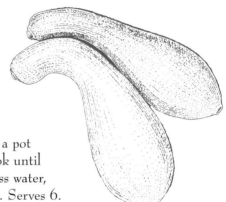

Place the squash and onion into a pot of salted water and bring to a boil. Cook until all is tender and mushy. Drain off excess water, add the butter and check for seasoning. Serves 6.

Scalloped Tomatoes

1   onion, diced
1   green pepper, diced
1   celery stalk, diced
3   Tbsp. butter

1   28-oz. can stewed tomatoes
2   tsp. sugar
     salt and pepper to taste
1   cup toasted bread cubes

Sauté onion, green pepper, and celery in butter until limp. Add the stewed tomatoes, sugar, salt and pepper. Place in a quart casserole and stir in toasted bread cubes. Heat in 325°F oven until hot through. Serves 4.

Fried Green Tomatoes

This way of fixing tomatoes is originally from Virginia although it didn't take it long to move further south and into the mountains. When I was a child my grandmother fixed fried green tomatoes for breakfast.

1	cup cornmeal	4-5	Tbsp. shortening
2	green tomatoes		salt and pepper to taste
3	tsp. sugar		

Slice tomatoes ¼ inch thick and sprinkle with salt, pepper, and sugar. Roll in cornmeal and brown in skillet with ¼ inch shortening over medium heat. Brown on both sides. Drain on paper towel. This will serve about 4 people and is very good with an omelet for breakfast. If you want to fry okra, yellow or zucchini squash, repeat the above process, leaving out the sugar. They all go well at dinner with baked pork chops.

POTATOES

Scalloped Potatoes

Serve these potatoes at a cookout or at any sit-down meal.

8-9	potatoes, peeled, thinly sliced and parboiled about 5 minutes	2	cups milk
		1	stick butter
1	cup flour		salt to taste

Grease a 9 x 13 inch pan or casserole dish and put in a layer of the potatoes. Dust with flour, add salt and dot with butter. Add another layer of potatoes, flour, salt and butter. If you have room, add a third layer of the ingredients. Pour the milk over everything, bringing the liquid level to the top of the potatoes. Place in a 350°F oven and bake about 45 minutes. Serves 12.

Oven-Browned Potatoes

6 medium potatoes
1 package ranch dressing mix

4 Tbsp. butter
salt to taste

Peel and cube the potatoes into bite-sized pieces. Put them into a pot of salted water and bring to a boil for just a minute. Drain and place in a roasting pan, dot with butter and sprinkle the ranch dressing mix over them. Bake in a 350°F oven until brown and tender. Serves 8.

Potato Puff

3 cups leftover mashed potatoes
1 small onion, diced
3 Tbsp. butter

1 cup milk
1 egg
salt and pepper

Sauté the onion in butter. Beat the egg and milk together and mix with the potatoes and onion. Pour into a greased quart casserole and bake at 325°F for 45 minutes. Serves 4.

Potatoes with Sour Cream and Chives

This dish is tasty with barbecued beef ribs.

2 lbs. potatoes,
  peeled and sliced
1 onion, sliced

2 cups sour cream
½ cup fresh chives, chopped

Bring sliced potatoes and onions to a boil in salted water. Remove from heat and drain. Mix sour cream and chives and layer the potatoes and sour cream mixture in a baking pan. Bake at 350°F for 30 minutes. Serves 4.

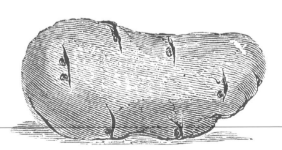

Twice-Baked Potatoes

6 baking potatoes
1 small onion,
     diced and sautéed
3 strips bacon,
     fried and crumbled

1 cup Parmesan or sharp
     cheddar cheese, grated
6 Tbsp. butter
1 cup milk
   salt and pepper to taste

Bake your potatoes in a 350°F oven until done, about 45 minutes. Remove and let cool. Cut in half and scoop out potatoes to leave a empty hulls. Mash the pulp and season well with salt, pepper, onion, butter, milk and bacon bits. Re-stuff the hull, top with the cheese and bake until the potatoes are hot and the cheese melted. Serves 8 or 10.

Baked Sweet Potatoes

Sweet potatoes are so good and sometimes forgotten. They are chock full of vitamins and minerals, and so versatile that they can be used in any of the recipes that call for a sweet squash such as butternut, candy roaster or pumpkin.

1 sweet potato per person
1 cup brown sugar
1 tsp. cinnamon
1 stick butter

Wash the potatoes and bake at 325°F for 1 hour. Cut them half way through in the shape of an X and push from the sides to pouf them up. Mix the brown sugar, cinnamon and butter. Heat and serve to the side.

Breads & Cereals

Breads & Cereals

FROM TOP: *Grist Mill in Cades Cove with customers' waiting room, 1924.*
Photograph of a natural mill race on Oconoluftee near Three Forks by George Masa.

As in years gone by, the Cataloochee kitchen incorporates a lot of cornmeal and other corn products in its menus. Corn was the staple of the south in lean years, easily grown on either steep mountain slopes or in the heat of South Georgia and it served both man and his animals. The grain kept well, needing only a corncrib for storage and cats to keep the mice away. The people used every particle of the plant, eaten fresh on or off the cob, ground fine to make cornmeal, ground coarser to make grits, parched corn like peanuts, lye-soaked corn to make hominy and sprouted corn to make moonshine. The dried fodder fed the animals and the shucks could be used to bottom chairs, stuff a mattress, or make a horse collar. Every community had its grist mill where corn was ground and payment was made with a "dole," or part of the ground meal.

Diversions from the daily work routine were few so mountain folk enjoyed turning work into a social event. In the spring there were workings where people gathered to help their neighbors clear new ground — the men did the clearing while the ladies cooked the midday meal and the children invented games to play. Or neighbors gathered for a barn raising or a house building, having fun while getting the job done. Corn shuckings could go on way into the night with lots of food, good music and chances for a young couple to "spark." A boy or girl who found a red ear of corn got to kiss whoever they chose, not all innocent fun, but full of imagination.

Breads & Cereals 95

Cornbread

Cornbread is a staple of our mountains. There are probably as many ways of fixing this all-purpose bread as there are cooks. Some like it thin and some like it thick. Some like it with lard and some like it with Canola oil. Some preheat the oven and others put it into a cold oven. I'm listing my preferences and a few of the variations.

Cast iron is the pan of choice for cooking cornbread. When you get a new pan, season it well according to the directions. It may take a while before the pan becomes sufficiently seasoned so that the bread drops out when turned over. Never wash a bread pan and don't use it for anything but bread. I return mine to the hot oven as soon as I have turned the bread out and never have a sticking problem.

2 cups Three Rivers Cornmeal Mix (*my preferred brand because it just tastes better*)	4 Tbsp. shortening, divided 1½ cups milk

Combine meal and milk with half of the shortening and gently blend. Do not over stir. Add the remaining shortening to a 10-inch iron skillet and pour in the batter. Shake the pan gently to get the shortening up around the sides and bake at 450°F until brown. When the bread is done, remove the pan and shake it to loosen the bread. Then invert the pan and the bread should drop out. Serves 6.

For variations try this . . .
1. Substitute mayonnaise for shortening in the batter
2. Add a small diced onion
3. Use ½ milk and ½ cold water
4. Substitute buttermilk for milk
5. Use only water as your liquid

Cornbread Salad (See Cookouts)

Mexican Cornbread

Add to basic cornbread batter
- 1 small onion, diced
- 1 small can whole kernel corn
- ½ cup cheddar cheese, diced
- 1 green pepper, diced
- 1 small chili pepper, diced
- 1 small tomato, diced

Fried Bread

You can substitute flour for cornmeal and it is just as good. This bread is especially tasty served with wild game.

2   cups Three Rivers Cornmeal Mix   shortening for deep frying
1   cup water

Pour enough oil into a skillet to make it about 1 inch deep. Set the skillet over medium-high heat to let it start getting hot while you make the batter. Just mix the meal and water together and spoon into the hot oil. Fry quickly on one side and turn it over until the bread is golden brown. Drain on paper towels. Serves 6.

Hush Puppies

Serve with trout or other fish.

2   cups Three Rivers Cornmeal Mix   ⅓   cup onion, diced
1¼ cups milk   ¼   cup green pepper, diced

Mix ingredients. Drop by spoonfuls into hot oil. Fry until golden brown. Remove and drain on paper towels. Serves 12.

Lazy Man's Bread

Just what it says — good bread for those who don't like to knead and roll out biscuits and clean up the mess.

2   cups self-rising flour   4   Tbsp. shortening, divided
1¼ cups milk

"Free heat" the oven to 450°F. Put 2 Tbsp. shortening into a 10-inch iron skillet and place in the heating oven. Meanwhile, combine all ingredients, mix and pour into the hot skillet. Bake until crusty brown, about 15 minutes. Serves 6.

Biscuits

2	cups self-rising flour	⅔-¾	cup milk
½	cup shortening		

Sift the flour and cut in the shortening. Add enough milk and mix until the dough leaves the side of the bowl. Too much milk makes the dough too sticky to handle and not enough makes the biscuits too dry. Biscuits will be lighter if you do not work the dough too much, just enough to get all the flour wet. Turn out onto a floured surface and gently knead the dough 2 or 3 times, bringing in a little flour off the table until all stickiness is gone. Roll out until about ½ inch thick. Cut with biscuit cutter of desired size. Place on greased cookie sheet and bake at 450°F until brown, about 20 minutes. Makes about 10 biscuits.

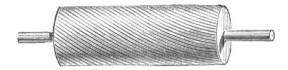

Spoon Bread

This was a traditional dish in Virginia where Mother was born. My grandmother served spoon bread at breakfast, lunch or dinner. She arose early every morning to make spoon bread or biscuits for breakfast, serving them with country ham and red-eye gravy or with country gravy or turkey hash. My, were we spoiled!

2	cups water	1	egg
1	cup Three Rivers Cornmeal Mix	1	cup milk
2	Tbsp. butter	½	tsp. salt

Stir the meal and the butter into the salted water and cook over medium heat until thick, stirring constantly. Remove from the heat and set aside. Beat the egg and milk together and combine all the ingredients, mixing well. Pour into a greased quart casserole and bake at 325°F for 45 minutes. Serve hot with plenty of butter. Serves 5.

Homemade Yeast Rolls

Bobby and Richard Blythe taught us to make these rolls when they were cooking for the ranch. The rolls are so good and not too complicated.

¼	cup shortening	1	egg, beaten
¼	cup sugar	1½	tsp. salt
2	cups scalded milk	5-6	cups sifted plain flour
¼	cup lukewarm water	2	packages yeast

Combine scalded milk, shortening, sugar and salt. Cool to lukewarm. Soften yeast in a small amount of lukewarm water. Stir and combine with cooled milk mixture. Add egg and about ½ the flour. Beat well. Add enough remaining flour to make a soft dough. Mix thoroughly and turn out on a lightly floured board. Knead about 10 minutes until smooth and satiny. Place dough in a warm greased bowl, brush surface lightly with melted shortening, cover and let rise in a warm place for 2 hours. Shape into rolls, cover and let rise till double in bulk, about 30 to 45 minutes. Bake at 375°F for 15 to 20 minutes until brown. Makes about 25 rolls.

Easy, Easy Rice

My Uncle Miller Alexander was the owner of a huge rice plantation in Louisiana, where they served rice almost three times a day. He taught us that rice is not hard to cook and can be made almost foolproof with little or no measuring.

1	pot of water	1	tsp. salt
	(4 or 5 cups,	1	cup rice
	makes no difference)		

Put rice into the salted water, boiling or not, makes no difference. Boil until tender, about 20 minutes. Drain through a colander. If not serving immediately, place the colander over boiling water then fluff with a fork before serving. The best rice to use is the extra-long grain, not the converted. It stays nice and fluffy and white. Tastes better, too. Serves 4.

Fried Rice

Growing up, we had steak and rice quite a lot because the cattle were raised on Hemphill Bald, and our freezer always had a good supply of beef. Remove some of the fat from the steak and render it out in a frying pan. Quickly sear the seasoned steak on both sides until you have the desired doneness: about 2 minutes on each side of a 1-inch steak for rare. Remove the steak and put cooked rice into the drippings and stir around until lightly browned.

Spanish Rice

6	slices bacon	3	cups cooked rice
¼	cup onion, diced	1	16-oz. can tomatoes
¼	cup green pepper, diced		salt and pepper to taste

Fry bacon and reserve 2 Tbsp. of the drippings. Sauté the onions and peppers until tender. Crumble the bacon and add the rest of the ingredients. Cook, uncovered, over low heat for 15 minutes. Serves 4.

Rice Pilaf

1	cup extra long grain rice	1	small onion, diced
3	Tbsp. oil	1	celery stalk, diced
	salt to taste	2	cups water
1	carrot, diced		

Heat the oil in a pot and add the rice. Stir the rice around to parch it and then add the onion, celery and carrot. Pour in the water and add salt. Place into a roasting pan, cover tightly and bake at 350°F for 1 hour.

Desserts

Desserts

Cataloochee Ranch puts on the finest spread of desserts ever seen.

Whether simple or sinful, desserts are a pleasant way to finish a meal. As a youngster I quickly learned that dessert has two ss's since I always wanted double helpings. Mr. Tom had but one requirement for a good dessert: every evening he would ask, "What's under the whipped cream tonight?"

Desserts are a way for skillful cooks to show off their skills. Mountain people use lots of fruits and berries, readily available in fields and on hillsides. When wild strawberries ripen in June, whole neighborhoods go to the fields to fill their buckets. At other times the same is true with blackberries, blueberries apples, raspberries and cherries. Taking cues from Mr. Tom, who was so good at getting guests into the hayfield, Miss Judy would entice the guests to go on berry picking expeditions. When the guests brought in the berries, Miss Judy made a jam of the berries that they had picked and presented a jar to each picker. In strawberry season Norman created his marvelous wild strawberry shortcakes . . . two layers of a special pastry, with loads of wild strawberries and plenty of _real_ whipped cream between the two then topped with more whipped cream and the biggest and best of the berries used to decorate the top.

Norman's Strawberry Shortcake

Pie Crust

2	cups all purpose flour, sifted	⅓	cup butter
½	tsp. salt	½	cup ice water
2	Tbsp. sugar		

For the Crust

In a mixing bowl, combine the flour, salt and sugar. Add the butter and work it with your hands until the mixture resembles coarse crumbs. Add the water, 1 tablespoon at a time, and work it in with your hands until you have a smooth ball of dough. Wrap the dough in plastic and refrigerate for at least 30 minutes. Place the dough on a lightly floured surface. Roll out the dough as close to a rectangle as possible and trim the edges with a knife to make them straight. This should make about a 12 x 8 inch sheet. Place the dough on a cookie sheet and bake in a pre-heated 425°F oven for 10 or 15 minutes or until lightly brown. Repeat the process for a second crust. Serves 10.

2	pints strawberries, sliced
	sugar to taste
1	pint whipping cream
4	Tbsp. sugar
1	tsp. vanilla

To Build the Shortcake

Sprinkle 2 pints of sliced strawberries with sugar to taste and let stand while you whip the cream. (If you are lucky enough to have wild strawberries, leave them whole, reserving the best for the top layer.) Whip until stiff 1 pint of whipping cream, adding 4 tablespoons of sugar and 1 teaspoon of vanilla about half way through. Spread the first short cake layer with whipped cream, then a layer of strawberries. Repeat the process for the second layer, reserving the biggest and best berries for the top to make an eye-appealing dessert. Let the cake stand for about 1 hour before slicing and serving.

Jane's Amber Sauce

This recipe goes back to Jane's grandmother and great grandmother before her. It turns ordinary vanilla ice cream into an incredible gourmet treat. It is so easy to make and stores for months in the refrigerator. All you have to do is pull it out and heat it in the microwave before serving.

1 cup brown sugar	½ cup butter
1 cup Karo syrup	1 cup heavy cream

Simmer sugar, syrup and butter for 10 minutes. Add cream. Stir. Ready to serve or to store in refrigerator. Serves 10.

Apple Crisp

1 28-oz. can of applesauce	1 tsp. cinnamon
½ cup sugar	dash of lemon juice
½ tsp. nutmeg	

Mix above ingredients in a quart casserole and top with the following mixture.

½ cup oatmeal	⅓ cup flour
½ cup brown sugar	¼ cup melted butter

Bake at 325°F until hot through, about 15 minutes. Serves 6.

Apple Float

You may also use rhubarb. If you do, cut it into small pieces and bake it in the oven with sugar until it is soft and mushy.

3	cups applesauce	1	tsp. nutmeg
1	cup sugar	3	egg whites
2	tsp. cinnamon		

Beat egg whites until they are stiff, adding ¼ cup sugar as they stiffen. Season the applesauce with the cinnamon, nutmeg and ¾ cup sugar. Bring the applesauce to a boil and then fold it gently into the egg whites. The hot applesauce will cook the egg whites and keep them stiff. Serve with ice cream or whipped cream. Serves 5.

Baked Apples

4	apples, peeled, cored and sliced	½	tsp. nutmeg
1	cup sugar	1	tsp. cinnamon
¼	stick butter		dash of lemon juice

Spread apples in a shallow baking dish. Sprinkle with the sugar, cinnamon, nutmeg, dash of lemon juice and dot with the butter. Bake at 325°F for 30 minutes.

For a variation on this, peel and core your apples, but leave them whole. Stand them on end in a dish and place the seasoning mixture into each hole. Serve 1 apple to each person.

Banana Pudding

6-8 ripe bananas, divided
1 box vanilla wafers, divided
2 boxes of instant vanilla pudding (the smaller size)
1 cup sour cream
   whipped cream

Slice the bananas and alternate wafers with bananas until a 2-quart casserole is almost full, saving some of each for later. Mix pudding according to directions on the box and add the sour cream. Pour over the wafers and bananas. Top with the saved bananas and line the edges of the casserole with some of the wafers. Serve topped with whipped cream and a red cherry. Serves 10.

Jane's Brickle Cream

Can be made in a trice and always gets rave reviews.

1 pint whipping cream
½ cup sugar
1 tsp. vanilla
10 oz. brickle bits
10 oz. milk chocolate morsels

Whip the cream with sugar and vanilla. Fold in brickle bits and chocolate. Spoon into a serving bowl or individual parfait dishes. Freeze for a few hours before serving. Will keep for days. Serves 8 to 12.

Jane's Brickle Pie

8 oz. soft cream cheese
2 cups heavy cream
10 oz. brickle bits
10 oz. milk chocolate bits
   chopped pecans or
   slivered almonds
1 9-inch pie shell

Whip the cream cheese. Whip the cream. Gently mix together. Fold in brickle bits and milk chocolate pieces. Place in pie shell. Sprinkle with nuts and freeze.

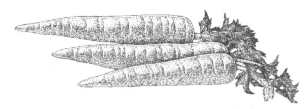

Carrot Cake

2	cups self-rising flour	3	large carrots, shredded
2	cups sugar	1	cup chopped walnut nuts
1	tsp. cinnamon	1	tsp. vanilla
1½	cups shortening	1	tsp. black walnut flavoring
3	eggs		

Sift together in a large mixing bowl the flour, sugar and cinnamon. Beat the shortening and eggs together and add them to the flour mixture a little at a time, mixing after each addition. Add the carrots and the remaining ingredients and mix well. Pour into a greased pan and bake at 350°F for about 45 minutes.

Topping

1	cup buttermilk	½	cup white sugar
½	tsp. soda	1	tsp. honey
½	cup brown sugar		

Mix together and bring to a hard boil. Spread on the cake while still hot.

Baked Custard

This is a very simple dessert that can be enhanced by topping with fresh fruit and whipped cream.

2	cups milk or cream	2	tsp. cinnamon
2	eggs	1	tsp. nutmeg
4	Tbsp. sugar	1	tsp. vanilla

Mix all the ingredients together then pour into individual custard cups that have been greased with butter. Place cups in a pan with ½ inch of water and bake at 325°F until set, about 45 minutes. Use this same recipe to make rice pudding by adding 1 cup cooked rice and ½ cup raisins. Serves 8.

COBBLERS

When you think about food in the mountains or in the South, one of the first items that comes to mind is cobbler. You can make cobblers out of almost any fruit — apples, blackberries, blueberries, strawberries, rhubarb, peaches, etc. Some cooks make a crust much like a piecrust (see below), while some make a topping more like a cake batter. A lot of the mountain people sweeten their biscuit dough a little and top the fruit with it before baking. With apple cobbler, you would want to use some cinnamon and nutmeg, but no matter how you make your cobblers, they are universally applauded.

Blackberry Cobbler

You may substitute any fruit or mixture of fruits.

2	quarts blackberries, fresh or frozen	2	Tbsp. butter
2	cups sugar	6	Tbsp. cornstarch

Place blackberries in 10 x 13 inch cake pan. Mix cornstarch and sugar and sprinkle over the top of the berries. Dot butter over the top.

Crust
2 cups plain flour
⅓ cup butter
½ cup ice water or milk
1 tsp. salt
1 egg, beaten

Sift flour and salt then cut in butter. Add water gradually to make a soft ball. Roll out on a floured surface. Cut into strips and make a lattice on top of the berries. Brush with 1 beaten egg and bake at 350°F until golden brown. Serves 10 to 12.

Blackberry Dumplings

Also use strawberries or blueberries.

1½	quarts blackberries, fresh or frozen	3	cups water
1	cup sugar	1	can biscuits (5 to a can, cut in half)

Bring berries and sugar to a boil in the water. Drop the biscuit pieces into the boiling berries and cook until done, about 20 minutes. Stir a little if the juice doesn't cover the dumplings. Serve hot with ice cream or whipped cream. Serves 6.

Damson Plum Pie

The Damson plum is becoming rare but you might find it at the mountain farmers' markets. It is a small purple plum that has a nice tartness to it and makes wonderful jam (See Jams and Jellies). You may also buy damson preserves in most grocery stores. On the mountain here, we have two trees that are probably 75 to 100 years old, and they have little trees coming on if we can protect them from the horses. The horses love the plums and gobble them as soon as they fall, but they also love to nibble on the trees themselves.

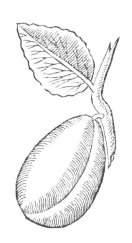

1	cup butter	1½	cup Damson plum jam (see page 161)
¾	cup sugar	1½	tsp. vanilla
8	eggs	1	pie crust

Cream butter and sugar. Beat eggs until light and add to first mixture, then add preserves and vanilla. Fill the crust and bake in a 325°F oven until brown. Serve with whipped cream or ice cream.

Candy Roaster Cake

Candy Roaster, a member of the squash family, is a wonderfully versatile vegetable and so easy to prepare. I guess you could even make candy out of it, although I have never heard of that. But, you certainly can prepare it as a vegetable, a pie, a cake and even as a butter for hot biscuits. For any of these Candy Roaster recipes, you may substitute pumpkin, sweet potatoes or butternut squash. There will be a small difference in taste but not too much.

3	cups sugar	1	tsp. soda
1	cup shortening	½	tsp. baking powder
3	eggs	¼	tsp. salt
16	oz. candy roaster,	1	tsp. vanilla
	cooked and mashed	1	tsp. cinnamon
	(preparation tips on page 84)	½	tsp. each cloves, allspice
3	cups flour		and nutmeg
		1	cup nuts, (optional)

Cream sugar and shortening. Add eggs and candy roaster and mix well. Add remaining ingredients as listed. Bake in greased and floured tube or Bundt pan. Bake 10 minutes at 350°F and then lower heat to 300°F and bake 55 minutes longer.

Candy Roaster Pie

2	eggs, lightly beaten	1	tsp. cinnamon
2	cups candy roaster,	½	tsp. ground ginger
	cooked and mashed	¼	tsp. ground cloves
¾	cup sugar	1	12-oz. can evaporated milk
½	tsp. salt	2	pie crusts

Preheat oven to 425°F. Combine filling ingredients in order given. Pour into pie shells and bake 15 minutes. Reduce temperature to 350°F and bake an additional 45 minutes. Cool and garnish with whipped cream. Makes two pies.

Chocolate Soufflé

Served with whipped cream, this is one of the world's most elegant desserts. You can bet that Dad loved his soufflé well covered with whipped cream. Quite sinful, but oh so good! And the tartness of the bittersweet chocolate is tantalizing.

3	Tbsp. butter	3	eggs, separated
3	squares Bakers	½	cup sugar
	Bittersweet Chocolate	1	tsp. vanilla
½	cup flour	2	cups milk
	dash of salt		

Melt the butter and chocolate in a double boiler. Make a roux by adding the flour and stir. Cook for about 5 minutes then begin adding the milk slowly, stirring until smooth and thick. Add the sugar. Remove from the heat and stir in the egg yolks. Add the vanilla and salt. Beat the whites until stiff and then fold them gently into the chocolate mixture. Pour into a buttered 1-quart casserole and set in a pan with 1 inch of water. Bake at 350°F for 45 minutes or until the top springs back when lightly touched. Serves 6.

Chocolate Upside-Down Cake

4	cups plain flour	8	Tbsp. cocoa
8	tsp. baking powder	2	cups milk
1	tsp. salt	8	Tbsp. shortening
3	cups sugar		

Topping

2	cups brown sugar	7	cups hot water
8	Tbsp. cocoa		

Mix the first 5 ingredients then add the milk and shortening. Spread mixture into two 9 x 13 inch pans. Mix the brown sugar and cocoa and sprinkle over the two pans. Pour 3½ cups very hot water over each pan. Bake at 350°F for 35 minutes. Check for doneness by dipping a spoon in the middle of one of the pans. If the syrup on the bottom comes out as dark as chocolate syrup, it is done. Use a large spoon and turn the cake upside down so the syrup is on top. Serve with whipped cream if desired. Serves about 20.

My Grandmother's Fruit Cake

This is a very old recipe that has been passed down through the family. Every Christmas, my sister-in-law, Jane, bakes these cakes because Brother Tom thinks, "It ain't Christmas without Grandma's fruit cakes."

¾ lb. butter	1 lb. raisins
1 lb. brown sugar	1 lb. currants
8 eggs	

Instead of using the first four ingredients below, you can buy the mixed fruits now available at Thanksgiving and Christmas in most supermarkets.

½ lb. orange or lemon peel	½ oz. ground cloves
½ lb. citron chopped fine	½ oz. cinnamon
½ lb. crystallized pineapple	¼ oz. nutmeg
½ lb. cherries	1 tsp. vanilla
½ lb. pitted dates	4½ cups flour
½ lb. blanched almonds	1 cup sherry
½ cup black molasses	1 cup brandy

Beat butter and sugar until light and creamy, then add thoroughly beaten eggs. Add raisins and currants coated with flour, then all other fruits, chopped and coated with flour. Then add the molasses and spices. Sift and add the flour, and, lastly stir in the sherry and brandy. (Wine may be substituted). Grease and flour tube cake pans or loaf pans, line them with two layers of wax paper (very important) and pour in the batter. Place cake pans in a large baking pan, add ½ inch of water and steam slowly for about 2 hours on top of the stove. Finish baking in 250°F oven for about 1 hour longer until done. The straw test is good for this, i.e. insert a clean broom straw and if it comes out clean the cake is done.

When the cakes are thoroughly cool, place them in cake tins and pour brandy over them. Let stand covered for about two weeks before serving.

Fruit Surprise or Dump Cake

Into a 9 x 13 inch pan, dump 1 can crushed pineapple and 1 can cherry or strawberry pie filling. Spread 1 box of yellow cake mix on the pie filling. Cut 2 sticks of butter into small squares and dot over the cake mix. Sprinkle with chopped walnuts. Bake at 350°F for 40 minutes or until brown. Serves 8.

Jane's Fudge Pie

1	stick butter	1	cup sugar
2	squares unsweetened chocolate, melted	½	cup flour
		1	tsp. vanilla
2	eggs, beaten	⅛	tsp. salt

Cream butter, melted chocolate, add sugar, flour, eggs, salt and vanilla. Beat together. Bake 30 minutes in 325°F oven. Serve with whipped cream. Serves 8.

Frozen Lemon Chiffon

1½	cups graham cracker crumbs	½	cup Realemon juice
2	12-oz. cans evaporated milk	½	tsp. vanilla
¼	cup sugar		

Chill milk until very cold. Sprinkle ½ of the crumbs into the bottom of 9 x 13 inch pan. Beat the milk until soft peaks form. Add lemon juice and sugar. Add vanilla. Pour into the pan and sprinkle remaining crumbs on top. Freeze and cut into squares to serve. Serves 8 to 10.

Old-Fashioned Stack Cake

This was the traditional mountain Christmas cake, sweet but not too sweet. The thinner the layers and the more of them, the better the cook. The most stacks that I have seen is nine. As a child, I remember Addie Sutton, one of our neighbors, coming every Christmas with a stack cake wrapped in wax paper and a sprig of holly tied at the top. That takes a lot of work! The

cake was also served at weddings where invited guests brought a layer before the ceremony. The mother of the bride then spread each layer with stewed apples, stacked the cake, wrapped it in a damp cloth and set it aside to await the wedding day. The more layers, the more popular the bride.

3 cups plain flour	½ cup shortening
½ tsp. baking powder	½ cup butter
½ tsp. cream of tartar	2 eggs
1 cup packed brown sugar	1 tsp. vanilla

Beat together the eggs, sugar, shortening, butter and vanilla. Sift together the dry ingredients and stir into the egg mixture. This will make a stiff dough. Divide the dough into 7 pieces. Grease and flour seven 8 inch cake pans. Line the pans with waxed paper then pat the dough balls real thin to fit the pans. Bake at 375°F until brown.

Filling

2 8-oz. packs of dried apples	1 tsp. nutmeg
5 cups water	¼ tsp. cloves
1 cup sugar	¼ tsp. salt
1 tsp. cinnamon	

Simmer apples in water for 45 to 50 minutes or until the apples are very soft. Stir in sugar and spices. Spread on the layers while still hot. Leave the top layer plain. Let stand a couple of days before serving, then slice thin and serve with whipped cream or ice cream.

Peach Fritters

These would go well with a luncheon or a brunch. You can also use any other fruit — bananas, blueberries or strawberries.

1½	cup plain flour	1¼	cup milk
1	egg, beaten	1	16-oz. can peaches, reserve the juice
½	tsp. salt		dash of lemon juice
½	cup sugar		
3	tsp. baking powder		

Mix the dry ingredients and then add the egg, peaches, milk and lemon juice. Spoon the batter into hot (400°F) vegetable shortening and fry until nicely brown. This will make about 8 fritters. Drain on paper towels.

Sauce

1	cup reserved peach juice	1	Tbsp. flour
¼	cup sugar		

Mix all the ingredients together and bring to a boil. Cook one minute then pour over the fritters.

Jessie's Pecan Pie

Jessie Jenkins was our chef for about five years in the 1980s and helped us increase the popularity of the cookout. He also gave us this delicious recipe for pecan pie. This pie would do well with a dinner that includes Roast Leg o' Lamb, Rice Pilaf, Sugar Snap Peas and Onion Casserole — a dinner not indigenous to the mountain region, but certainly elegant and deserves this pie.

1	9-inch pie shell	1	tsp. vanilla
1	cup sugar	2	eggs
½	cup melted butter	6	oz. chocolate chips
½	cup plain flour	1	cup pecans, walnuts or black walnuts

Beat eggs, add sugar, flour and butter. Fold in chips, nuts and vanilla. Bake at 350°F for 45 minutes. Let stand 6 hours before slicing. Do not refrigerate.

Prune Cake

This cake holds many fond memories for me and my siblings. One year brother Tom was working in New York, Alice was also in New York attending design school and I was in Germany. Miss Judy thought that birthdays must be celebrated with birthday cakes. She first tried shipping a two-layered chocolate cake to Tom on his birthday, but the U.S. Postal Service made a mess of it. Then she thought of the durability of the Prune cake, both for shipping and its shelf life. My cake arrived in perfect shape, and the long overseas trip only served to enhance the flavor

3	eggs	1	tsp. cinnamon
1	cup vegetable oil	2	tsp. vanilla
1½	cups sugar	1	cup buttermilk
2	cups flour	1	cup prunes,
1	tsp. soda		cooked and chopped
2	tsp. baking powder	1	tsp. black walnut flavoring
1	tsp. salt		or 1 cup chopped
1	tsp. nutmeg		black walnuts
1	tsp. allspice		

Sauce

1	cup sugar	1	tsp. vanilla
½	cup buttermilk		dash salt
½	tsp. soda	2	Tbsp. white corn syrup
½	cup vegetable oil		

Blend sugar and oil and add beaten eggs. Add dry ingredients alternately with buttermilk. Add vanilla, prunes and nuts or flavoring to the mixture. Mix well. Pour into 2 greased 8-inch square pans. Bake at 350°F for 45 to 50 minutes. While cake is baking, boil sauce mixture until it is foamy and rather caramel colored. After removing from the oven, prick hot cake in several places and pour sauce over while both are hot.

Rhubarb Cake

Rhubarb is a very popular fruit here in the mountains, and is delicious in pies and cakes or just plain baked in an oven with sugar and butter and served on hot cornbread.

1½ cups brown sugar	1 tsp. soda
½ cup shortening	1 cup buttermilk
1 egg, beaten	½ cup rhubarb, cubed
2 cups all purpose flour	

Cream the shortening and sugar. Add the egg, flour, soda and buttermilk and fold in the rhubarb. Spread in a greased 9 x 13 inch pan and bake at 350°F for 30 to 35 minutes. Sprinkle the top with ½ cup white sugar mixed with 1 tsp. cinnamon. Serves 10.

Rhubarb Pie

2 9-inch pie shells	2 beaten eggs
1½ cups sugar	1 Tbsp. butter
3 Tbsp. flour	6 cups rhubarb,
½ tsp. nutmeg	cut into ½ inch pieces

Spread the rhubarb in the pie crusts. Blend sugar, flour, eggs, nutmeg and unmelted butter. Beat until smooth. Pour over rhubarb in pie crusts and bake at 450°F for 10 minutes, then at 350°F about 30 minutes. Serve topped with whipped cream.

Sweet Potato Pudding with Whiskey

1	pint cream or milk	⅔	cup brown sugar
3	medium sweet potatoes, peeled	1	Tbsp. melted butter
		2	tsp. cinnamon
3	eggs	½	cup whiskey or rum

Grate potatoes into cream to keep from darkening. Add beaten eggs, sugar and cinnamon. Add melted butter and whiskey. Bake at 325°F 1 hour or until firm and brown. Serves 6.

Strawberry Mousse

2 12-oz. cans evaporated milk
1 cup sugar
1 pint of strawberries, fresh or frozen, mashed
   dash of lemon juice

Chill milk thoroughly, then beat until stiff and add the sugar, berries and lemon juice. Blend and pour into a 9 x 13 inch pan to freeze. When about half frozen, stir with a fork to fluff it up. Return to the freezer until fully frozen and serve. Serves 8 to 10.

Trifle

Miss Judy loved serving this dessert for a little more "uptown" atmosphere.

1	small pound cake	2	oz. brandy or rum
	raspberry jam		whipped cream
1	box instant vanilla pudding, prepared according to directions on box		

Slice down through the pound cake to make 12 thin slices. Lay half of the slices in a 9 x 13 inch pan. Spread on a layer of the raspberry jam. Add the brandy or rum to the pudding and spread a layer on the jam. Spread a layer of whipped cream over the pudding and repeat the process, making sure that you end with whipped cream on top. Let this sit for about an hour before slicing into squares to serve. Serves 8 to 10.

Zebra Cake

This is a universal favorite for children and adults alike! Until recently you could only buy chocolate wafers once a year when Nabisco made them, but the wafers are now available year round at most supermarkets.

1   package Nabisco's Famous Chocolate Wafers
2   pints whipping cream, whipped very stiff
      with a ½ cup sugar and 1 tsp. vanilla

Put a generous amount of whipped cream on the first cookie, place the second on top of it and add more cream. When you have 7 or 8 cookies stacked, lay them down on an oblong or rectangular dish like a log. Continue adding wafers and cream to the log. When you have used all the wafers, spread a generous amount of whipped cream over the entire log to completely cover it end to end and top to bottom. Refrigerate for 2 or 3 hours, then slice on a 45 degree angle to give the desired zebra effect.

Cookouts
& Camp Cooking

Cookouts

Cataloochee Ranch is famous for the outdoor buffet table.

Cookouts

Soon after Cataloochee Ranch opened on Fie Top in 1939, we initiated cookouts. In those days Sunday lunch was a large, truly southern meal consisting of either fried chicken and all the trimmings or roast turkey with cornbread dressing, giblet gravy, etc. This was the meal called "dinner," while the evening meal was "supper." Sunday night supper included pan-fried hamburgers, corn on the cob, sliced tomatoes and cottage cheese, a casserole of some sort and tossed salad. The hamburger buns were yeast rolls, made from scratch and cut to fit the size of the hamburgers. Alice and I patted out the burgers every Sunday afternoon and made the salad dressing according to Miss Judy's recipe (see below). Mr. Tom cooked the burgers in a long-handled frying pan on an open fire behind the ranch house. He never let the guests forget that he raised the beef on Hemphill Bald and nurtured it to maturity. If an innocent guest asked for a well-done hamburger, Mr. Tom would stop what he was doing, turn around to gaze at the unsuspecting person and give a little lesson on the care that went into raising succulent beef cattle. He always concluded his spiel with, "And you want me to burn this little thing up?!"

Over the years, our cookouts have grown in popularity and frequency, and we now offer them three evenings a week as well as three lunches a week. As Miss Judy taught us, we put a lot of effort into making the outdoor meals well balanced, nutritious and appealing to the eye. The staff takes great pride in the appearance of their dessert and buffet tables, and the picnic-style dining tables are covered with checkered cloths and attractive centerpieces.

Patsy Gaddis, our head chef, runs the evening cookouts. Patsy came to work here in housekeeping when she was 17, and later moved to the wait staff. Over the years she worked her way into the kitchen, first as a cook's helper and dessert maker, then on to breakfast and lunch cook and now as head chef. Always at Patsy's side at the grill is her invaluable co-chef, Tom John Aumen, who built the complicated cookout rig where we serve our dinners. Tom John married my sister, Alice, and after Miss Judy retired, Tom John, Alice and I took care of ranch management. As our cookouts increased in popularity, Tom John came up with the design for the outdoor buffet table. The top is wooden and has holes for the warming pans, silverware, salad bowl and all the condiments. Under the warming compartments are places to put the sterno to keep the food hot. At the end of this table, his homemade stainless steel charcoal grill turns out the burgers, steaks, ribs or chicken.

Another one of Tom John's designs is the "kitchen" that goes to the woods for pack trips. This traveling kitchen has room to carry all the food, utensils, propane, stoves and tarps to take care of twenty people for four days. It is pulled by a truck that carries the wood, horse feed and duffle. Tom John does all the cooking for these trips except for the prep work that we do before the trip begins.

Tommy Dale Woody, Patsy's brother, is our breakfast and lunch cook and responsible for the lunch cookouts. Both partners of this sister-and-brother combination have a fine imagination for food and an extremely strong work ethic.

Cookouts can be served inside, of course, which we do when it rains, but food seems to taste better when cooked and eaten in the fresh air.

In this section I also include some of the food that we take on pack trips, foods that taste delicious when cooked over an open fire.

Backbones & Spareribs

Pork backbone and its attached ribs have a delicious flavor and are so much fun to eat with your fingers — make sure there are plenty of napkins available. The ribs are also delicious when basted with the tangy BBQ sauce.

Along with spareribs, we offer Roasted Chicken Breasts and usually accompany the meat with Corn Pudding, Baked Sweet Potatoes, Green Bean Casserole, Tossed Green Salad with choice of three Dressings and Assorted Desserts. Serve with the BBQ sauce of your choice. Offer a mild sauce along with a tangy one, such as the following sauces Tom and Jane serve at their steam-engine barbeques.

3   ribs per person
    salt and pepper

1   large can tomato juice

Season a whole rack of ribs with salt and pepper. Pour tomato juice over them, cover and bake at 300°F for about 4 hours. Then place on the grill to finish off. As you are serving, slice the ribs apart.

Tom & Jane's Southern BBQ Sauce

A favorite BBQ sauce, this also makes a fine basting sauce for chicken, fish and pork. Keeps for weeks in the refrigerator if tightly sealed.

2   Tbsp. butter
6   Tbsp. cider vinegar
¼   cup water
1½ cups ketchup
2   Tbsp. Worcestershire sauce
¼   tsp. Tabasco sauce

1   tsp. garlic, finely chopped
3   Tbsp. peanut or corn oil
    salt and pepper to taste
2   Tbsp. sugar
1   lemon

Combine all ingredients except the lemon in a saucepan. Add juice of the lemon. Cut the lemon into quarters and add it. Heat thoroughly without boiling.

Tom & Jane's Tangy BBQ Sauce

1 cup strong coffee	¼ cup lemon juice
1½ cup Worcestershire sauce	2 Tbsp. sugar
1 cup ketchup	2 tsp. salt
¼ lb. butter	cayenne pepper to taste

Mix all ingredients and simmer for 30 minutes. Keeps in the refrigerator a long time.

Barbecued Beef Ribs

To go with the beef ribs, a sample menu would be Baked Potatoes with Sour Cream and Butter, Cornfield Beans, Fresh Corn on the Cob, Scalloped Tomatoes, Tossed Green Salad with Choice of Dressings, Hot Homemade Rolls and Assorted Desserts, including Fresh Watermelon.

1½ large beef ribs per person
1 32-oz. can tomato juice
   salt, pepper and minced garlic

Place ribs in baking pan and sprinkle with salt, pepper and minced garlic. Pour tomato juice over them, cover and cook in a 300°F oven for 6 hours. Remove, place on the grill and add BBQ sauce as desired. Again, it is a good idea to offer two kinds of BBQ sauce, one sweet and one tangy.

Beef Marinade for Steak

1	cup soy sauce	1	Tbsp. ginger, ground
¼	cup brown sugar	1	Tbsp. lemon juice

Mix all ingredients and spread on the steak for about one hour before grilling. You may also use this marinade on the beef ribs.

Baked Beans

1	#10 can of pork and beans	¼	cup brown sugar
½	cup onion, diced		dash of liquid smoke
½	cup green bell pepper, diced		

Place all ingredients in roasting pan. Bake at 350°F for about 1 hour. If desired, you may add a couple of slices of bacon on the top before baking. Good flavor! Serves about 15.

Broccoli & Cauliflower Salad

1	bunch broccoli, cut up and steamed until tender	1	head cauliflower, cut up and steamed until tender
½	cup onion, chopped	½	cup cucumber, chopped

Mix all ingredients well and serve chilled with the salad dressing of your choice. Below is the recipe for Miss Judy's Sunday night dressing, very easy to make. Serves 10.

Miss Judy's Vinaigrette Dressing

⅓ cup vinegar
⅔ cup olive oil
1 Tbsp. minced garlic
2 tsp. sugar

2 tsp. ketchup
salt and pepper
½ tsp. Italian Seasoning

Combine all ingredients and mix well. Store in a jar with a tight-fitting lid so you can shake it well before serving.

Jane's Vinaigrette

⅓ cup good balsamic vinegar
⅔ cup extra-virgin olive oil
1-2 pinches of Coleman's powdered mustard

salt and generous portion of freshly-ground black pepper to taste
3 cloves garlic, minced

Combine ingredients. Mix well.

Grilled Rainbow Trout

With trout we generally serve Baked Pork Chops. The meats are accompanied by Baked Potatoes with Sour Cream and Chives, Fresh Green Beans with Okra, Squash Casserole, Yeast Rolls, Tossed Green Salad and Choice of Dressings and Assorted Desserts.

Sprinkle desired number of 6-inch rainbow trout with lemon pepper and dot with olive oil. Wrap in foil and place on the grill for about 5 minutes on each side. Serve off the grill.

Marinated Grilled Chicken Breasts

1	chicken breast per person boneless, skinless	½	cup honey mustard
		4	Tbsp. teriyaki sauce

Mix the honey mustard and teriyaki sauce and spread on the chicken breasts. Marinate for about 1 hour. Place on the grill about 5 minutes per side, basting with the marinade occasionally.

Coleslaw

1	head of cabbage, chopped fine but not miniscule	3	Tbsp. sweet pickle relish
		1	Tbsp. sugar
¼	head of purple cabbage, chopped	¼	cup vinegar
2	carrots, diced	½	cup mayonnaise
1	celery stalk, diced		salt and pepper to taste

Mix well and keep tasting until satisfactory. Serves 12.

Cornbread Salad

This recipe comes from Denny Sutton and is a different and tasty way to use leftover cornbread, which is always in abundance in mountain homes. If you don't have leftovers, make fresh bread.

Make cornbread according to the recipe on the package. I prefer Three Rivers Cornmeal mix. Crumble the bread into a large bowl. Dice any vegetables you would like in a salad except for lettuce: onions, celery, carrots, cucumbers, tomatoes, green peppers, radishes, squash or whatever you think of. Pour in a large jar of store-bought ranch dressing. No special brand recommended. Mix and refrigerate overnight. Serve garnished with lettuce leaves.

Deviled Eggs

6	eggs, hard-boiled		salt and pepper to taste
¼	cup mayonnaise	6	slices bacon,
1	Tbsp. honey mustard		fried crisp and crumbled

Cut the eggs in half and place the yolks in a small mixing bowl. Mash the yolks with a fork, then add the mustard, mayonnaise, salt, pepper and 3 slices of crumbled bacon. Mix well and taste for seasoning. With a teaspoon carefully return the yolk mixture to the eggs, being careful not to break the whites. Top off with the rest of the crumbled bacon. Serves 6.

Stuffed Butterfly Pork Chops

With stuffed pork chops we might also offer Marinated Chicken Breasts on the grill (see above), accompanied by Scalloped Potatoes, Steamed Asparagus, Candy Roaster Puff, Broccoli and Cauliflower Salad and Assorted Desserts.

1   pork chop per person,
      cut 1-inch thick
1   box Uncle Ben's Wild
      Rice mix, cooked

salt and pepper to taste
seasoned flour for
      dredging the chops

Carefully slice the pork chops toward the bone to make a pocket. Stuff the cavity with the wild rice mixture and salt and pepper both sides. Dredge the chops in the flour and brown them in olive oil on each side. Place the chops in a pan with a rack in it and pour water in the bottom. Cover and bake at 350°F about 1 hour. Place on the outside grill to finish them off.

Party Potatoes

*Like his brother, Cookie,
George Wood liked to cook, especially
for a party. He came up with this
caloric recipe to feed a crowd and all would leave happy and full.*

10 lbs. potatoes	1 bunch green onions
½ lb. butter	12 oz. shredded cheddar cheese
½ lb. bacon	salt and pepper to taste

Peel and cut up the potatoes (Got some help?). You may use canned potatoes instead and would not have to cook them as long. Melt the butter in a large roaster and toss in the potatoes. Salt and pepper them. Cover tightly with tin foil and place in a 325°F oven for about 1½ hours or until fork tender. While the potatoes are cooking, fry off the bacon until it is crisp, and chop the onions. Remove the potatoes and sprinkle the crumbled bacon, green onions and cheddar cheese on top. Return to the oven for about 10 minutes. Serves about 20.

Potato Salad

3 lbs. white potatoes	1 green pepper, diced
1 cup Dukes mayonnaise	3 Tbsp. mustard
2 hard boiled eggs, diced	1 small onion, diced
½ cup sweet pickle relish with juice	2 celery stalks, diced
	1 tsp. celery seed
	salt and pepper to taste

Peel, cube and cook the potatoes in salted water until almost tender but not too done. About 10 minutes. Drain and let cool. Add all the ingredients and mix well. Taste for satisfactory seasonings. Serves about 12.

Pulled Pork BBQ

Pulled Pork BBQ is quite often served on a lunch cookout, and with it might be BBQ chicken, Baked Beans, Potato Salad, Coleslaw, Tossed Salad, Green Onions from the garden, Pickled Beets and an assorted Dessert Table.

1   pork loin
    salt, pepper and
      minced garlic to taste

a mild BBQ sauce
a Tangy BBQ sauce

Place pork loin in roaster, cover, and cook at 250°F for 12 hours. When cool, pull the pork apart and season with salt, pepper and garlic. Add the BBQ sauce. Cover and return to a 350°F oven for an additional hour. Serve with the mild BBQ sauce and a tangy one.

Pinto Bean Casserole

This dish goes well with a hot dog cookout, and sometimes we use it on a Poor Man's lunch buffet served indoors. A Poor Man's Buffet would include Potato Soup, Vegetable Soup, Pinto Bean Casserole, Garden Greens, Macaroni and Cheese, Tossed Salad and assorted Desserts.

    cornbread batter
2   28-oz. cans pinto beans,
      undrained

½   cup onion, sautéed
½   cup ham, chopped
½   cup cheese, shredded

Make a cornbread batter according to the directions on the package. Add the onions, ham and cheese to the pinto beans, top with the cornbread and bake at 450°F until golden brown. Serves 10.

Camp Cooking

FROM TOP: *Sam Woody kneeling while Larry Caldwell serves a trail meal on Mt Sterling in 1940.*
Faithful Rube, the pack horse, hoofs it into the first night's camp in the Cataloochee Valley, 1941.

Camp Cooking

Mr. Tom and Miss Judy held their
first packtrip in 1935 for The American
Forestry Association. Over the years the foods we serve on
these trips have been tested and refined to the point where
they are tasty, nutritious, compact and need little if any refrigeration. On the long trips (10 days), the first night's menu
always consists of fresh meat (steak usually), corn or potatoes,
salad, bread and dessert. On subsequent nights we serve foods
needing no refrigeration. On the fourth day, someone supplies
the group with welcome hay for the horses, clean clothes for
the riders and fresh meats and vegetables.

Today we lead shorter forays into the Great Smoky
Mountain National Park, customized according to what the
guests want, such as whether they want to carry everything
on a pack horse or would prefer an auto-accessible camp that
can be supplied by vehicle. When my friend Cookie and I go
out to do volunteer work on the Appalachian Trail, we carry
everything including our work tools on our two riding horses
and live very comfortably.

We lighten our packs by taking only changes of under-
wear. If we get wet we let the clothes dry on us and we have
never caught a cold. We break breakfast eggs into a plastic jar

and store them in the creek at night along with squeeze butter. We always have a good axe and fire starter and cook over a small fire to save carrying a stove. We fix one-pot meals and take instant mixes for drinks to save carrying heavy liquids.

Packtrip Coffee

Fill a small coffee pot about ¾ full of cold water. Pour coffee grounds on top of the water to make a mound about ¾ inch high. Put the pot on the fire, bring it to boil and let it boil about 30 seconds. Remove the pot and dribble cold water down the spout and around the rim to settle the grounds to the bottom. A gentle hint: make sure the pot is on the fire with the handle to the outside. Saves burnt fingers.

Practice making this coffee until you can tell by eye the exact amount of coffee to use.

Roasted Corn

1½ ears of corn ears per person,   butter
    still in the husk   salt
    water

Good for BBQ's or any cookout and also good when camping. Turn back husks of the corn and remove the silk. Leave the husks on and soak in salted water about 1 hour. Carefully insert butter and a little more salt, then replace the husks around the cob and place on the grill to roast about 10 minutes, turning frequently. You may also shuck the corn completely, dot with butter and a little salt and wrap in tinfoil. Then place it on the grill or in a 425°F oven.

Camp Stew

A great one-pot meal that includes soup as a first course! This is a meal that you can fix on your second or third night out in the woods, since it requires no refrigeration.

2   cans Armour Roast Beef
     with Gravy
4   potatoes
1   large onion

2   celery stalks
3   carrots
     salt and pepper to taste

Peel and prepare the vegetables, cutting them into bite-sized pieces. Place the vegetables in a pot with a lot of water, add a goodly amount of salt and pepper and bring to a rolling boil. Cook about 10 minutes or until just getting tender (If you are camping at high altitudes, you have to allow more time for things to cook, so adjust to your altitude).

Everyone can dip out their own delicious cup of soup (or pot likker) to whet their appetites for dinner. When the excess liquid has been dipped off, add the canned meat and gravy and let simmer until everyone is hungry. A fresh-made pan of cornbread (see below) tops this meal off to perfection. Serves 4.

Pedigreed Hot Dogs

Good on a holiday cookout.

1   pack of jumbo hot dogs
8   slices of bacon
8   slices of cheese

Slit each hot dog and stuff the entire length with the cheese. Wrap each dog with a strip of bacon and secure with a toothpick. Grill until bacon is done or bake in the oven at 350°F until done.

Pork Loin Sandwich for the Woods
with Potatoes Baked in Ashes
& Cornbread Over a Fire

8   slices (uncooked) wafer thin pork loin
1   large onion, sliced
2   yellow squash, sliced
    green beans, parboiled about 5 minutes and sliced lengthwise
    salt, pepper and butter

1   medium potato for each person, greased and wrapped in foil.

Tear off a fairly large piece of tinfoil and lay a slice of pork on it. Salt and pepper it a little. Place a couple of onion slices then some squash slices then some sliced green beans, then some more onion slices. Sprinkle with salt and pepper and drizzle the butter on each layer. Place the other slice of pork on top and wrap the entire sandwich tightly. Put this into the freezer until the morning you leave for your camping trip. I did not put potatoes on the sandwich because they turn black when you freeze them.

After you get to camp and make the fire, let it burn down until there are just good hot coals. Pull some hot ashes out of the fire and put the potatoes in them and cover with hot coals. You don't want the potatoes to get too hot because the skin crusts up and prevents heat from getting to the centers so they don't cook through. The potatoes should take about 40 minutes to cook, but you need to test them with a fork for doneness before serving.

You make cornbread in the woods with the same recipe as you would use at home but the difference is the pan. Look in some flea markets and find an omelette pan, one that is hinged in the middle and made of heavy aluminum. Put your cornbread mixture in one side of the pan that has been well greased, fold the top over it and place it on the fire, not too hot. When one side is well browned, turn the pan over and brown the other side. When you put your bread on the fire also lay the pork sandwich on the grill and turn it when you turn the bread. The bread and the sandwich will each take about 15 minutes.

One and One Half + One Half = Two

We came on this camping idea when we got lazy and didn't want to spend all our time over the fire, cooking and cooking. In this meal you cook a simple meal in the evening and you make more than enough so that you can then make breakfast the next morning with just a simple addition. Therefore the name. This serves 3, supper and breakfast.

One and One Half

1 can Hormel ham patties (6 to a can, fully cooked)
6 medium potatoes
1 large green pepper, sliced (optional)
1 large onion, sliced
   salt and pepper
4 Tbsp. shortening

Peel and slice your potatoes. Put them in the pan with the shortening and salt and pepper and fry them a few minutes. Add the sliced onion and pepper and cook until almost done, turning often. Cut the ham into bite-sized pieces and add to the onion and potatoes, cover, and cook until the ham is hot through. This serves 3 people supper. Serve it with cornbread or with Lazy Man's Bread but save what is left over.

The Other Half

6 bacon slices
6 eggs
½ cup sour cream (optional)
½ cup shredded cheese (optional)

The next morning fry the bacon and set it aside. Reserve about 3 Tbsp. of drippings. Beat the eggs well with salt and pepper, adding the sour cream if desired. Put the leftovers from last night into the middle of the fry pan and pour the eggs over the top, lifting the edges for the eggs to run under. Cover and cook on low heat until the eggs are set. Top with the cheese if you want.

Campfire Potatoes

This recipe calls for a Dutch Oven, which is too heavy to carry on a horse or in a backpack, so you would save this for a trip made by vehicle.

Peel and quarter potatoes and put into a Dutch oven. Lay strips of bacon over the potatoes and salt and pepper to taste. Replace the lid, place the oven in hot coals and cover it with hot coals. Cook about 30 minutes or until done.

Potatoes & Onions

Another idea for a campfire meal that would give you the starch to go along with pork loin sandwiches.

4	potatoes, sliced	salt and pepper
1	large onion, sliced	3 Tbsp. shortening

Place the shortening in a frying pan and add the potatoes, salt and pepper. Cook them a little, turning occasionally, and then add the onions. Cook these until they are fork-tender, about 15 minutes. If you don't want so much onion in the meal, leave them out of the pork sandwich. Serves 4.

Wild Game & Foods
From the Woods

Wild Game & Foods From the Woods

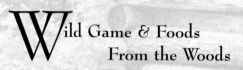

FROM TOP: *Mr. Tom with Uncle Charlie Rich (left) and his brother, Frank Rich.
Mr. Tom with famous cattle killing bear.
When not building fences, pickin' the banjo or rounding up stray cattle,
Cookie Wood serves as head hog hunter for the Ranch.*

Bear hunting has a long and venerable heritage in the mountains and to this day mountain people will angrily defend their right to hunt bear. But in olden times the hunt was very different from what it is today. Before the advent of radio tracking collars for the dogs, two way radios and ATVs (All Terrain Vehicles) for the hunters the bear had a sporting chance of getting away unscathed. In those days all the hunters were assigned a specific job, some to stand at a spot such as a gap where the bear might cross when chased by dogs. This place was called a "stand." Other hunters would release the dogs in hopes of striking a fresh track, and the hunt was on. If a bear crossed a stand and the hunter there missed the shot, he ceremoniously lost his shirt tail to his guffawing fellow hunters. Mr. Tom lost his shirt tail at what we now call "Tom's Stand," the home of brother Tom and his wife, Jane.

Recently, another type of hunt — for Russian wild boar — has taken a more serious turn. Russian wild boar were introduced to this area in the 1930s for hunting purposes and were kept penned except for the hunt. In the same era before the Great Smoky Mountain National Park was formed mountain families let their cattle, sheep and razorback hogs range free on the high mountains to be rounded up in the fall. But not all were caught and those that weren't soon mated with escaped Russian boar, producing feral hogs that destroy woods and pastures. In one night, in his quest to find grubs to eat, one hog can turn over enormous amounts of sod. If not turned back quickly, the grass dies, leaving the mountain ripe for erosion by wind and rain. Hogs reproduce at an alarming rate, six or eight to a litter, two or more litters a year. No natural predator can keep them in check now that the wolf and panther are gone from this area. And bear hunters will not risk their prize bear dogs to these fierce creatures.

Our own hog hunter, Cookie Wood, has dedicated a lot of his night-time hours to making a dent in the hog population. Armed with night vision scope and binoculars he waits patiently for hours, not moving and hoping the fog won't roll in to hide his prey. Sometimes wild pigs come just after dark, sometimes in early morning, sometimes on one side of the mountain, sometimes the other side, and sometimes not at all. So far though he has shot upwards to 80 hogs, bringing a lot of meat to neighbors and friends.

Wild Boar

Wild boar can be a tough and stringy meat, but when cooked long and slow and marinated at least overnight it is delicious and gives one a feeling of pioneer eating.

Marinade

2	cups Soy sauce		½	cup lime juice
½	cup corn syrup		2	Tbsp. ground ginger
1	cup water			

Place the roast in a large, covered pot and pour on the marinade. Turn to coat all the meat with the mixture. Refrigerate and let stand at least overnight, two days is better. Remember to turn the roast occasionally to make sure all of it is coated

Drain off the marinade, rinse the roast, then fill the pot with enough water to cover. Add an ample amount of salt, pepper, garlic salt and a small amount of hot pepper. Bring to a boil then reduce the heat to simmer. Simmer until the meat is very tender when pricked with a fork, about 2 or 3 hours, longer for the hams and shoulders. The hams and shoulders can then be baked until brown in a 350°F oven and the smaller pieces can be painted with a BBQ sauce of your choice and baked about 10 minutes.

Squirrel Dumplings

3-4 squirrels, cut up
1 qt. water

2 Tbsp. butter
salt and pepper to taste

Boil the squirrels with salt, pepper, and butter about 45 minutes. Remove from the broth and pull meat from the bone. Reserve the broth.

Dumplings
2 cups plain flour
1 tsp. salt

1 egg
1 cup of squirrel broth

Mix flour and salt, stir in the egg and add the hot broth. Roll out on floured board and cut into 2 or 3 inch strips. Drop the strips into the boiling stock. Cook 10 minutes on medium heat, then add the squirrel meat. Check for seasoning.

Groundhog

Parboil the groundhog about 45 minutes. Change the water and continue boiling with 1 tsp. baking soda, 1 Tbsp. vinegar, 1 Tbsp. salt, 1 small hot pepper and 1 small onion, sliced. Cook until tender, about 1 hour. Drain and dredge with seasoned flour, place in a roaster and bake until brown.

Venison Roast

Sprinkle the venison roast liberally with salt, pepper and garlic powder. Place in roaster with about 3 cups of water. Cover tightly and roast at 325°F for 3 hours. To serve, make a gravy of the drippings, slice the roast and pour a little gravy over it.

Bear Liver

This is the most delicious of all livers! Old bear hunters claim that most bears they kill don't have a liver since the first man to get to the kill takes it and leaves.

Dredge the liver in flour seasoned with salt and pepper. Sauté slowly in bacon drippings and brown on both sides. Smother with sautéed onions if desired.

Bear Roast

This is Miss Judy's original recipe for bear roast, so popular with our guests and Mr. Tom that he decided to transport some to New York for a dinner for the Honorary Tarheels. The HTH, a group of journalists who had written articles about North Carolina, were rewarded with two weekends a year, one on the coast, the other at Cataloochee Ranch. The guests abandoned all inhibitions and constraints and had a jolly good time. The biannual meetings were attended by the governor and other NC powers that be. At this one-and-only New York meeting, the guests came back for seconds and thirds until all the bear meat was gone.

1	large bear roast	a few needles of rosemary
	salt and pepper	½ bay leaf
¼	cup oil	2 Tbsp. ketchup
1	clove garlic, crushed	2 tsp. Worcestershire sauce
1	medium onion, chopped	½ tsp. celery salt
2	celery stalks, chopped	½ tsp. dry mustard
1	small dried red pepper	

Remove all fat from the bear roast and rub generously with salt and pepper. Sear the meat on all sides in a large pot with a small amount of oil. Add water a quarter the way up the roast. Put in the remaining ingredients, cover tightly and simmer for about 3 hours, adding water if necessary. When the roast is very tender, remove it and set aside. Into the drippings, add a flour-and-water paste and stir to the desired thickness for gravy. Adjust seasonings. Slice the roast very thin and ladle on the gravy that has been strained. Excellent served with wild rice or fluffy long-grained rice.

Rabbit Dressing

This favorite recipe comes from Colleen Rich, a native of Maggie. Her husband, Butch, is an avid rabbit hunter, so she has no problem getting meat. Wild rabbit is best, as it is all dark meat and not sweet. If this is not available, most grocery stores carry rabbit.

Boil the rabbit in salted water about 30 minutes or until almost tender. Drain and save the liquid to make the following dressing.

2	cups Three Rivers Cornmeal Mix	4	Tbsp. butter
4	Tbsp. shortening	2	Tbsp. rubbed sage
1½	cups milk		salt and pepper to taste
1	celery stalk, diced	2	eggs
1	small onion, diced	2	cups rabbit stock

Mix cornmeal, shortening and milk and bake at 450°F to make the cornbread. You can use leftover breads, but be sure half is cornbread. Crumble the bread into a mixing bowl. Sauté the onion and celery in the butter and add to the bread, plus all the remaining ingredients. Spoon the dressing into a 9 x 13 inch pan. Cut the rabbit into nice serving sizes and place on top of the dressing. Bake at 350°F for about 45 minutes.

Branch Lettuce

Springtime in the mountains is the time for gathering delicious fresh edibles such as branch lettuce. Gathering greens is a time-honored social event best enjoyed by taking a good friend with you who knows what wild plants look like. Branch lettuce is a watercress that only grows in certain streams and branches in late April and early May. Carry a sandwich, a bottle of wine and a collecting bag and plan to spend the day hiking, looking at early spring flowers, and picking.

When you come to a stream that grows branch lettuce, pick off the tender leaves and take home a lot. You can use the lettuce in a regular tossed salad or in the mountain tradition, fix it "kilt" (killed). To do this, fry about 3 or 4 strips of bacon, saving the drippings. Mince a little onion, sprinkle bacon bits and salt and pepper over the lettuce, then gradually pour the piping hot drippings over it while someone tosses it. Serve immediately.

Creasy Greens

Creasy Greens are a cress with a stronger taste. They are sold in our local grocery stores in March and April, but the ones that you find in cornfields around the area are smaller and much tastier.

Wash the greens well and cut into pieces using the stem and the leaves. Season water with salt and pork side meat and boil the greens until tender, about 10 minutes. Drain and serve. Good with fried trout and potatoes.

Day Lilies

Gather the unopened orange day lily buds. Wash and drain. Plunge in boiling, salted water and cook about 5 minutes. Season with butter.

Poke Salad

Poke is a weed that appears in abandoned fields, especially where rubbish has been burned. It is fairly widespread. Check your flower book to make sure you are getting the right weed.

Pick young, tender shoots that have small green leaves on them. No roots! Wash well and cut into about 1 inch pieces. Parboil about 10 minutes in three different waters and add salt to taste to the last water. Then you can either fry them with eggs or roll them in seasoned cornmeal and fry to a light brown.

Stinging Nettles

The hardest part of this recipe is gathering the nettles. The plants protect themselves with little bristles that leave a nasty sting when you touch the plant. But, with a good pair of gloves and long sleeves you can collect nettles, which taste a little like spinach when cooked. After they are cooked, there is no sign of the bristles.

Clean and wash the leaves and slice them. Then, plunge into boiling salted water and cook about 5 minutes. Drain and season with butter.

Traditional Ramps and Eggs

2 lbs. ramps and tops, cleaned,   2 Tbsp. bacon drippings
     and cut into 1-inch pieces   3 eggs
1 tsp. vinegar   salt to taste

   Parboil the ramps about 5 minutes with a tsp. of vinegar. Drain
well and put into a fry pan with the bacon drippings. Add beaten eggs and
salt, and stir well while cooking. When the eggs are done, you are ready
to serve.

Tom Alexander's Ramp Soup

*Given the native power of raw ramps, this is a surprisingly mild
potage. Ramps calm down a lot with cooking.*

1 lb. potatoes,   1 large onion, sliced
     peeled and sliced   2 qts. chicken stock, or 1 qt.
1 lb. ramp bulbs,   each chicken and ramp stock
     peeled and chopped   2 Tbsp. butter

*(Note: the water in which ramp greens have been boiled for about 10 minutes
can be used instead of the bulbs and is actually much more flavorful.)*

   Sauté the ramps and onion in the butter until the onion is clear.
Then add the potatoes, the chicken stock and ramp stock and simmer,
covered, until the potatoes are very soft. Puree the vegetables in a blender
or food processor or, if you prefer, just mash them, and restore to the
stock. Salt and pepper to taste. This is good poured over a slice of bread
or cornbread in a bowl, French country-style.

Ramps

What, pray tell, are ramps? Something that goes on and off the interstate? Something you drive around and around to get to the top of a parking garage?

No, we are talking about a wild leek known as *Allium trioccum*, valued for its underground bulb, and leaves which appear in spring but disappear before the plant blooms. Growing on the north sides of our mountains in rich woods, ramps are at their best when the leaves are about five inches tall.

The joy of ramp season — early April to early May — is as much in gathering the plant as in the results on the table. Go to the woods when the sun is shining and Bloodroot, Dutchman's Breeches, Squirrel Corn and various species of Trillium are in full bloom. Pack your sandwich and a bottle of wine, get your plastic bag and a digger and head for the nearest ramp cove. It is a social event, so take a friend and enjoy the day.

When you return, sit on the lawn and clean your ramps, cutting the bulbs and leaves into small pieces. As you are cleaning the ramps, cut a little higher up on the bulb to get some of the meat to go with the roots. If you have a good location that ramps like, you can plant these bulbs and have your own ramp patch. I have one that spreads far down the hill. Now, wash the ramps and their leaves thoroughly and parboil in lightly salted water with a teaspoon of vinegar (to kill their powerful smell) for about five minutes, then drain.

The traditional way to prepare ramps is to fry them in bacon fat and gradually add enough eggs to make the dish green and yellow. Eat ramps with cornbread and fried potatoes or fish. You can also make a very tasty hot potato soup, substituting ramps for onions or excellent hashed-brown potatoes with sautéed ramps. Or, use your imagination.

Even in this area, ramps have a bad reputation for the odor they leave on the breath. Students have been sent home from school after eating raw ramps. But natives swear that when ramps are cooked with a little vinegar, little or no scent remains.

Recently, ramps have received a lot of publicity from ramp festivals in the mountains and national televised cooking shows, resulting in an alarming depletion of the ramp population. It takes about five years for ramps to reach maturity, and they only grow in secluded northeast-facing moist woods. The Indians dig them by leaving a portion of the bulb in the ground so that the ramp regenerates. Ramp diggers take note and follow this wise conservation method!

Pickles, Jams, Jellies & Cataloochee Punch

Pickles, Jams, Jellies & Cataloochee Punch

Miss Judy preserving fruits and vegetables in the outdoor cannery, 1935.

Years ago in September when the elderberries got ripe, Miss Judy collected a goodly amount of them, read a recipe for elderberry wine and proceeded to follow the instructions with her "winery" being the little room adjacent to the kitchen where the hot water heaters are kept. But, something was not quite right, and one day there was a large explosion whereupon elderberry wine in the making was scattered all over the kitchen and into the big room. Never again, she said. So, Miss Judy began experimenting and found out that a tasty jelly could be made of the little purple berries. Thus was the beginning of a fine tradition. Not only do the guests love the homemade jams and jellies served at every meal, but they find them a wonderful present to take home as gifts.

Today, Patsy and her brother, Tommy Dale, make case upon case of all sorts of jams, jellies and pickles in the spring before we get busy and usually have to make another run sometime during the summer. The rare varieties, elderberry, damson plum and candy roaster butter are at the top of the list for gifts, but blackberry, blueberry, peach, strawberry and combinations of these fruits are not far behind. Homemade pickles and relish are also very popular. Pick some up on your way out the door and enjoy!

Bread and Butter Pickles

I watched my mother many times making pickles from cucumbers from the garden. She would make dishpans full, jarring them for later use.

8	cups cucumbers, thinly sliced	1	stick cinnamon,
2	cups onion, thinly sliced		crushed into pieces
2	Tbsp. salt	2	cups vinegar
2	tsp. celery seed	2	cups sugar
1	tsp. turmeric		

Combine cucumbers and onions. Stir in salt. Let stand for 1 hour, or longer if convenient. Drain off all the liquid. Put into a pot with vinegar, sugar, celery seed, turmeric and cinnamon. Boil for 20 minutes. Vinegar varies, so before putting into sterilized glass jars, check for taste. If too tart, add more sugar. The pickles should have a fine sweet-sour-spicy flavor, which is better a week or more after they are made.

Freezer Coleslaw

This is more like a cabbage relish than slaw, but it is so good.

1	head cabbage, chopped fine	2-3	carrots, grated
1	green pepper, chopped fine	1	tsp. salt

Syrup

1	cup vinegar	1	tsp. celery seed
2	cups sugar	1	tsp. mustard seed
½	cup water		

Add the salt to the cabbage mixture and let it stand for 1 hour. Drain the cabbage. Combine the ingredients for the syrup and boil it for 1 minute. Cool. Pour cold syrup over all, mix and freeze.

Mango or Apple Chutney

4	cloves garlic, crushed	10	slices pineapple, drained
10	cups mangoes or apples, cubed	1	Tbsp. ground nutmeg
2	cups onions, chopped	1	Tbsp. cinnamon
2	lbs. brown sugar	1	Tbsp. ground ginger
3	cups vinegar	1	Tbsp. cloves
1	cup fresh lime juice	1	Tbsp. salt
2	lemons, chopped, peel and all	1	tsp. freshly ground pepper
	peel of 2 oranges	1	drop Tabasco sauce
	peel of 1 grapefruit	1	cup pitted prunes or dates

Put garlic, mangoes or apples, onion, sugar, vinegar, and lime juice in a saucepan and simmer for 10 minutes. Add the remaining ingredients and cook until the fruit is soft, about 20 minutes. The chutney can be kept in the refrigerator for about 6 months without sterilization. Makes 8 pints.

Green Tomato Pickle

6	lbs. very green tomatoes, sliced ⅛ inch thick	1	vial lime from the drugstore
2	gal. water	1	lb. sugar
		1	qt. vinegar

Spice bag in cheesecloth consisting of
1 Tbsp. allspice
1 Tbsp. cloves
1 Tbsp. mace
1 Tbsp. white mustard seed

Soak tomatoes in lime with just enough water to cover for 24 hours. Drain and soak in cold water 4 hours, changing water every hour. Drain and place in a pot. Bring the mixture of sugar, vinegar and spices to a boil and pour over the tomatoes. Let stand overnight. Bring the mixture to a boil for 1 hour, then seal in jars.

Pepper Relish

4 cups onions, finely chopped	10 green tomatoes, chopped (optional)
4 cups cabbage, finely chopped	6 red peppers, chopped
12 green peppers, chopped	½ cup salt, sprinkled over the vegetables

Let stand overnight, then rinse and drain.

6 cups sugar	1½ tsp. turmeric
1 Tbsp. celery seed	4 cups vinegar
2 Tbsp. mustard seed	2 cups water

Pour over the vegetable mixture, heat to a boil and simmer for 3 minutes. Pack into sterilized jars and seal. Makes 8 pints

Pickled Beets

1 gal. small beets, whole or sliced, cooked	2 cups vinegar
4 cups sugar	3 cups water
	3 Tbsp. pickling spice

Mix sugar, vinegar and water in boiler. Use cheesecloth to make a bag of pickling spice. Let boil for 4 or 5 minutes. Add the beets. Bring to a boil, then let cool and stand in the liquid for 1 hour. Seal in pint jars.

Squash Pickles

8	cups squash, sliced	2	tsp. celery seed
8	cups onions, sliced	4	cups sugar
3	green peppers in rings	1	tsp. turmeric
½	cup salt	2	tsp. mustard seed
5	cups vinegar		

Combine squash, onions and peppers. Fill the pan with ice and sprinkle salt over it all. Let stand for 3 hours. Combine the rest of the ingredients and bring to a boil. Pack the squash, etc. in pint jars, pour the liquid into the jars and seal. This recipe is also very good if you add cauliflower, green tomatoes and zucchini squash.

Apple Butter

1	gal. unsweetened applesauce	1	Tbsp. allspice
3	cups sugar	2	cups apple cider
¼	cup cinnamon	¼	cup lemon juice
1	Tbsp. cloves		

Combine all ingredients in a roasting pan. Cook in the oven set on 325°F for 1 hour or until thick. Stir frequently.

Blackberry Jam

You can use the same recipe for strawberry and blueberry jams.

5	cups crushed berries	1	box Sure-Jell (fruit pectin)
7	cups sugar		

Stir Sure-Jell into the blackberries. Make sure that the pot is amply big to allow for a full rolling boil. Bring the berries to a full boil, stirring constantly. At once add the sugar and boil hard for 1 minute, always stirring. Remove from the heat. Skim off the foam and ladle jam into jars. Screw on the lids and process in a boiling water bath for 5 minutes, or cover with ¼ inch of melted paraffin and let cool.

Peach Jelly

Miss Judy never wasted a thing, as evidenced by this recipe.

When you peel peaches for serving, never discard the peelings or the pits. Place them into a pot with enough water to cover and bring to a boil. Cook for about 15 minutes to get the full flavor and the essence of the fruit. Strain and measure your juice. For every 3 cups of juice you use 4½ cups of sugar, 1 box of Sure-Jell and ¼ cup of lemon juice. Bring the juice, the Sure-Jell and the lemon juice to a boil, then stir in the sugar. Boil for 1 minute, stirring all the while. Remove from the heat and skim off the foam. Pour jelly into jars and seal with melted paraffin.

Candy Roaster Butter

As we have said, there are many uses for this versatile squash. October is the perfect time to buy a candy roaster, for they are ripe and keep quite a while without refrigeration. (Refer to page 84 for preparation tips.)

1 gallon candy roaster, cooked and mashed	1 Tbsp. cloves
3 cups sugar	1 Tbsp. nutmeg
¼ cup lemon juice	1 Tbsp. ginger
¼ cup cinnamon	2 cups apple cider
	1 box Sure-Jell (fruit pectin)

Mix all of the ingredients except the fruit pectin. Bring to a boil and cook for 1 minute. Remove and add the Sure-Jell. Put into sterilized jars. Melt paraffin and spoon about ¼ inch on top of the candy roaster butter.

Damson Plum Jam

In early October, we can gather the plums off our two damson plum trees on the place. We have to be quick to get them before the horses do. We shake the trees to make the plums fall and then pick them off the ground, because the trees have very long thorns. When you get the plums home, squeeze each one to pop the seed out and then you can either make jam right away or freeze the fruit in amounts equal to a run of jam.

6	cups plums	½	cup water
8	cups sugar	1	box Sure-Jell (fruit pectin)

Mix the plums, Sure-Jell and water and bring to a boil. Then add the sugar and cook for 1 minute. Put into jars and seal with paraffin.

Elderberry Jelly

The elderberry bush blooms in middle June with a beautiful cluster of white florets. Up here on the mountain, the berries are getting ripe in middle September. There are two varieties, one brilliant red and the other deep maroon to almost black but they have the same flavor and can be mixed. Just pick them by breaking the entire cluster from the bush.

3	cups elderberry juice	1	box Sure-Jell (fruit pectin)
4½	cups sugar	¼	cup lemon juice

To obtain the juice for your jelly, snip the large stems from the berries and place them in a pot with just enough water to cover. Bring to a boil and cook for about 15 minutes, then strain the juice through a cloth. For one run of jelly, measure 3 cups of the juice into a pot along with 1 box of Sure-Jell and the lemon juice. Bring this to a boil and stir in the sugar. Bring back to a boil and boil hard for 1 minute, stirring constantly. Remove from the heat and skim off the foam. Pour into hot jars. Wipe off any spills from the rim and seal with ¼ inch melted paraffin. The remainder of the juice can be canned in jars. To do this, bring the juice to a boil and pour into hot jars. Seal and put aside for making more jelly later on.

At the still in 1941.

Cataloochee Punch

Now here is how you make it

4 cups lemon juice (at least 2 cups should be fresh squeezed)	3 quarts moonshine
	3 quarts water (to start)
	1½ Tbsp Angostura Bitters
3 cups sugar	

Mix all items in a large container the day before serving. Slice rinds of the squeezed lemons and mix in. Chill 24 hours. Dilute with additional 2 quarts water at serving time. Serve in a large punch bowl with ice and lemon rinds.

Cataloochee Punch

Miss Judy was a firm believer in using what is on hand, adding a few ingredients and a goodly amount of imagination, and coming up with a new idea. In this case, she took mountain moonshine and created a punch so tasty and innocent looking that many a guest has asked, "What hit me?" the next day. This punch is used on any festive occasion, but was invented to celebrate Mr. Tom's birthday. The recipe will make an ample amount for 50 people.

When we speak of moonshine, we remember with fond memories the days when moonshine making was a fine and respected art in the mountains, although according to the authorities it was illegal. Dad had asked his neighbors not to put their stills on his property, since he didn't want to blatantly break the law. But, one morning in the fall after a lot of leaves had come down during the night, a column of smoke indicated that a still had been set up not too far from the ranch house. Now Mr. Tom was not one to pass up an opportunity, and he could see how everyone would benefit from his idea. He asked his guests at the breakfast table if they had ever seen an authentic moonshine still and, of course, they all said no. Then he asked if they would like to see one and take home a little souvenir, and most said yes. So soon they had each rider mounted on a saddled horse and blindfolded. The riders were led around and around and up and down and eventually they arrived at the still. In the meantime, Mr. Tom had advised the still's operators of his scheme and they were game for it. Everyone prospered from the adventure. The still operators gained from sales, the guests enjoyed an event never to be forgotten and Mr. Tom collected rent for the horse ride.

Stories about this punch are legion. We thought you would enjoy Bettina Shackelford's version.

Once upon a time, and a long time ago it was, Alice Honey (Alice Aumen) invited me to help make Cataloochee Punch for Mr. Tom's birthday. Each year that birthday was an occasion of high celebration, levity and fun. I was quick to say yes.

I had never tasted Cataloochee Punch, but out on the porch the big glass bowl had always looked inviting and refreshing. My husband George said it was wonderful, so I went off to learn one of the mysteries of the mountain, how to make Cataloochee Punch.

Cataloochee Punch! That is what we were making on a fine August morning, sitting on the Ranch House porch with a big bowl and a few ingredients — a bottle of Realemon juice, some real lemons, a small bottle of Angostura bitters, a pitcher of sugar syrup and a big jug of white lightning, beautifully clear and beaded. I'd heard that was the way white was supposed to look, so we obviously had the right stuff.

A good splash of white went in the bowl, a tad of lemon juice, and syrup. We took a little taste, kind of harsh and not too tasty. Alice Honey added more white and some of the other stuff. We stirred and tasted. Getting better. The sky was so blue with only a puff of a cloud and the sun etched the tops of all the trees.

There was nowhere near enough for everybody, but Alice Honey explained that we were making a concentrate and water would be added before serving guests. Thus, more white went into the bowl and more of the other stuff, too. We stirred and tasted. Hey, getting pretty good. The sun was warm, a little too warm, but still a lovely day. My doubts were gone. It was getting toward lunch, so we hurried a bit, adding and stirring and tasting. Really smooth.

George would be expecting lunch. Alice Honey said not to worry, the punch was about ready. We just threw in the last bit of everything, gave it a good stir, tasted one last time. Perfect!!!! Nice, but it sure was getting hot.

I headed for the old red jeep and started home. I meandered past the barn and down the road, but after awhile I didn't seem to be going anywhere. I stamped on the gas pedal and there was a sort of lurch but no headway. Strange. After a few futile attempts, I got out to see if I could find the problem. Aha, there it was. I was wedged up against the gate. How did I get that far so fast? I couldn't open the gate because the fender was stuck through the wire. I crawled back to the jeep, couldn't get it started. Oh, I was in the passenger seat. Out and around, in again and back up, trying not to take the gate with me. Out and around again to open the gate. It worked. Back in and drive through. Back out to shut the gate. It seemed a long walk back, but Mr. Tom said always leave gates the way you find them, open or shut. This gate was kind of bent and that is the way I left it. Back in the jeep and on to the Shackelford cabin. George was waiting for lunch. Too bad. I folded up on the nearest bed for the rest of that beautiful day.

That evening at the ranch, when they brought out the punch pitcher and poured our mixture into the big glass bowl, the ice really melted fast; actually I think it smoked a little.

Cataloochee Punch! I can't drink it now, don't even like to smell it, but that sure was a beautiful day.

Remedies That Work

Miss Judy was the daughter of an Army surgeon and she gained quite a bit of medical knowledge from her father, but it was from her mother, affectionately known as "Miss Ducky," that she learned household remedies for routine household ailments. For the common cold Miss Ducky's Hot Toddy is probably the only cure known to the modern world, and for violent nausea, the "epizootics" as Miss Judy called it, there is the famous Magic Potion.

As children we all had our fair dose of these ailments and the remedies never failed to work. The best thing about the Hot Toddy was that one of the requirements for it to work was for the patient to be in bed for the evening. Mother would bring the hot drink to us and sit while we sipped it. You would sleep like a log and wake up the next morning feeling completely well and ready for what the day would bring. Whenever the "epizootics" hit us, we were treated to the Magic Potion and again the gentle care, consideration and concern helped a lot in making us well. This is tried and true and we use it today religiously.

Photograph of virgin country at Three Forks Basin by George Masa.

Miss Ducky's Hot Toddy (*for the common cold*)

1	mug water	1	tsp. sugar
	juice of 1 lemon	2	oz. bourbon
1	tsp. ground ginger		

Heat the first four ingredients in the microwave until boiling. Remove and add the bourbon. The patient should be in bed ready for the night, then you serve the hot toddy immediately. Even teetotalers have taken readily to this cure-all.

Magic Potion (*for nausea*)

juice of 1 lemon	1 egg white, beaten till foamy
(not out of the bottle)	1 glass crushed ice
	sugar to taste

Pour the lemon juice, egg white and the sugar over the ice and let the patient sip it through a straw. The heat of the hands will melt the ice and make the potion go down nice and slow.

Body Odor Cure

This cure for body odor came from Alethea Wood, a true mountain lady who died before I could gather more of her cure-alls. The plant to use is Angelica, known as hog root here in the mountains, and it is a member of the parsley family. It grows well in our rich, damp woods and is easy to spot, being about 4 feet tall and having an umbrella like cluster of greenish white flowers. The stem is smooth, dark purple and the stalks of the upper leaves have a swollen basal sheath.

Dig the plant to get the roots. Boil the roots in water then wash the offending parts of the body in this liquid. The result is immediate and lasts almost forever.

Photograph taken from Charlie's Bunion toward Mt. Leconte by George Masa.

Index